Self Help With Anxiety – Gen Z

Go from 'Adulting do not recommend' to 'Adulting like a pro': Relationships, Financial worries, Career decisions, Social media and friendships

Jennifer Kyndnes

Table of Contents

Introduction

Whenever you start to feel overwhelmed by the reality of an unknown future, I hope you can remember that today used to be one of those days that you worried so tirelessly about. Now, here you are, on the other side of that unknown, successfully making it through each moment, one breath at a time. And the fact that you're still breathing and finding light along the path is proof; your unknowns have not defined you. Even here, there is more to you. –Morgan Harper Nichols

Anxiety is one of those human emotions that we all dread to experience; it's that niggling feeling you get when you're in a situation that you're not quite sure how to handle. More often than not, the longer the uncertainty remains in you, the more that feeling grows until it becomes a large, growling creature that has you cowering before it. Most people can't tell you exactly when their worries grew into stress and then finally became anxiety. The unfortunate truth about life is this: It's impossible for anyone to go through life without ever experiencing fear, stress, or anxiety to some degree. Our human nature is to fear the unknown because we want to protect ourselves in every way possible, at all times. Anxiety finds its root in that fear, and that fear is a normal and, dare I say, healthy part of what makes us wholly human. You always want to know what you are getting yourself into or what will be expected of you at any given moment. No one wants to be found lacking in capabilities or cast out from a group. Fear is meant to help us survive and thrive in the various environments and situations we find ourselves in as we try and navigate life. We can only do that if we know how to use fear without letting it overwhelm us and debilitate us.

Although we all experience anxiety at various points of our lives, each person's anxiety is triggered by different things, and the intensity of your anxiety ebbs and flows depending on a number of factors. For example, if you are going for your first-ever interview for an academic or employment opportunity, then your anxiety will be high because you're stepping into unknown territory. You don't know what to expect, and you may be worried that you've prepared all the wrong things and you will mess up the interview completely. But you find that as you go for your second, third, and fourth interviews, you're less anxious. You're starting to get into the groove of those environments and you're getting a better understanding of what is expected of you, so you are better prepared each time. So, although you are facing the same situation over and over again, your level of anxiety in that situation and your response to it keeps changing because of external factors like your preparedness, your confidence in your ability to navigate that space, and your familiarity with that particular situation.

An overwhelmingly common experience that we all have with anxiety is that feeling of isolation. For a lot of us, going through life as a person that is more prone to experiencing feelings of anxiety can make you feel like you are the odd man out, the only one struggling to navigate aspects of life that others seem to be breezing through. Feeling like you cannot find relief in others by confiding your struggles and emotions to them because they won't understand can add to your anxiety. Finding yourself in this space can be incredibly challenging, not only because it's an uncomfortable mental state to be in, but because that discomfort transfers to your body.

It's a commonly known fact that our minds and bodies are intricately connected. It's therefore not surprising that the discomfort of anxiety not only affects our minds but extends to the body as well. Our brain is made to be in constant communication with the body so that all our bodily functions keep running as they should. So, when your brain becomes aware that you are in distress for some reason or another, it naturally communicates that to your body. There are common physical symptoms or sensations that mark the presence of anxiety in our bodies, but each person's physiological response is a combination of different symptoms or sensations that present themselves at varying intensities. For some people, their anxiety is marked by a weakness in the knees or sweaty palms and shortness of breath. For others, feeling anxious makes their throat dry up and their vision blur, or it makes them feel like a wormhole has suddenly appeared in their stomach.

In my younger years, whenever I had to present a project in class or speak in front of more than two people, my mind would suddenly go blank and my heart would pound at the speed of light, and the pounding would be louder than a 50-piece marching band on parade day. As the years progressed, the sensation of being anxious morphed into this sudden feeling that someone had poured ice cold water down my back, and it keeps evolving as I move through life and find myself exposed to new environments and foreign stressors. Your brain may recognize that what you are feeling is anxiety, but the physical sensation that accompanies that recognition may change with time or according to different anxiety triggers. The onset may be slow, or it could hit you like a ton of bricks out of nowhere. It differs from person to person and circumstance to circumstance. Being anxious is not a static state because the triggers for it are not static either. It may feel like it's something you constantly experience if you are often under stress, but the truth is that each experience you have with feeling anxious is new, and that means that you can choose how you interact with your anxiety every time it shows up.

The Illogical Shame of Being Anxious in an Ever-Changing World

We live in a world that is constantly changing and developing in new and unexpected ways. When you consider that anxiety is often described as a vague fear or discomfort of the unknown and the lack of control one has over said unknown, it becomes easier to understand why so many people suffer from anxiety, and you start chipping away at the idea that you are alone in your experiences with anxiety. Once you come to view anxiety as your body's way of waving a red cautionary flag at you, you begin the journey of interacting differently with anxiety, and you may even find yourself feeling validated in your experiences with it.

Being anxious is an isolating, overwhelming, and scary emotion to experience. Sometimes the anxiety can become so intense that you find it difficult to perform simple daily tasks because you can't bring yourself to focus on completing them or because you'd rather procrastinate than face performing a task that you know will bring back those all too familiar and unwelcome sensations that mark your anxiety. Having your life negatively affected by anxiety is a normal and common experience that almost everyone on the planet goes through, but people don't talk about these experiences because it's like an admission of failure or weakness on our part. We all want to be seen as well-adjusted members of society, and no one wants to be perceived as the person who can't bring themselves to wash the dishes or finish their passion project because they're crippled by anxiety. So, we all suffer in silence instead of sharing our struggles and helping each other through them.

Fortunately, you are not alone in your struggles with anxiety. According to an article published in The Lancet in 2021, research showed that about 298 million people suffered from anxiety disorders (Santomauro et al., 2021). With the recent global pandemic, this number is estimated to have leaped to around 374 million. The fear of an unknown disease and the uncertainty of how it would affect our health, finances, how we engage with each other, and what a post-pandemic world would look like certainly was fertile ground for everyone's anxiety to spike. And the mandatory isolation certainly did not help. It was difficult to be stuck at home with all these new fears swirling around your mind, knowing that everyone was just as uncertain and as scared as you were. Even now as we try to navigate life after the pandemic, we are experiencing real time changes to the social, financial, and political landscape on a global scale, and so the anxiety still ensues. Trying to wrap your head around all of that while simultaneously having to worry about completing your assignments and projects and having to clean your space or meal prep can be too much for anyone to handle.

Understanding the Spectrum of Mental Health

Before we go further on your journey to healing your mental health, it's important to distinguish the different levels of mental distress you may experience. This distinction is important if you're going to understand what it is you're going through, where you land on the mental health spectrum, and how you can apply the necessary tools toward reframing and managing your feelings.

The first thing is to learn the difference between worry, stress, and anxiety. Worry is an emotion that you feel when you're concerned about the future and find yourself dwelling on negative thoughts. The emotion is usually fleeting and tends to go away once you've taken the necessary steps to deal with your concerns. Worry stays in the mind and normally doesn't translate to any physical reactions in the body. Stress is step two on the worry ladder. There are a few differences between worry and stress, the first being that your body has a physiological response to the stress. Secondly, stress is usually caused by some external factor or stressor that is out of your control. When that happens, your body responds by releasing hormones that gear you up to get active and handle whatever threat you're being exposed to. Stress can be acute, meaning that it's short-lived and usually ends when you've dealt with the stressor. It can also be chronic, and that happens when the external stressor lingers for a while without a solution or when you're constantly under stress due to a number of different stressors that keep you in a stressed state for some time. Finally, anxiety is a lovely concoction of both worry and stress that shows up in both the mind and the body. Because of this, anxiety can be challenging to overcome, because you have to deal with both the cognitive and physiological aspects of it.

Being anxious doesn't mean that you suffer from an anxiety disorder. Like I said earlier, anxiety is something that people experience all the time. After all, we all live in a high-paced world where constant stressors seem to be the order of the day, every day. When your anxiety becomes overwhelming and it starts to affect your ability to take part in everyday life like you used to, it becomes a disorder. Once your anxiety gets to the level of being disordered, you might want to consider getting help from a professional to help you deal with it before it morphs into other disorders and escalates into other mental health concerns.

You Can Shine a Light in the Tunnel: Living a Fulfilling Life in Spite of Anxiety

I hope that as you read through this book, you begin looking at your feelings of worry, stress, and anxiety as a valid and normal reaction to the times we live in. I hope that you will start to consider your anxiety in a new light and you start being gentle and more patient with yourself as you go through the journey of building a toolkit to help you deal with your emotions on a cognitive and physiological level. There is nothing wrong with you or with how you're interacting with the world. No matter where you find yourself on the spectrum, you can take control of your anxiety. Yes, you read that right. Not only can you take control of your anxiety, but you can also learn how to harness it to improve your performance in the very same situations that gave you the most intense cognitive and physiological sensations of anxiety.

I know that when you are in the midst of an anxiety episode, it can feel like you are enveloped, and you cannot imagine escaping that overwhelming feeling, much less leaning into it to improve how you deal with life's unexpected jump scares. But what if anxiety is not the foreshadower of doom that you have thought it to be? What if you can find ways to work with your anxiety instead of running from it or being held captive by it? What if I told you that within you lies all that you need to overcome the negative effects of anxiety, and all you need is a little guidance on how to unlock those inherent skills and resources?

Anxiety is first and foremost an emotion, and like any emotion, it can be overcome. We all have the potential to rise above our anxieties and live a full and rich life in spite of our fears. It may not seem like it is possible to do this when you are in the thick of a particularly intense anxiety attack, but that is why I am here to teach you how to overcome your anxiety. It will require strategic action and patience with yourself, but it is possible.

This book aims to help you understand what anxiety is and how it works in your body. Once you understand what you are dealing with, it becomes easier for you to identify your anxiety triggers and develop personalized and effective strategies to deal with anxiety and stress. It is common to feel like you do not know where or how to start creating these strategies for yourself, and you can easily become overwhelmed if you do not have the guidance you need to get you started on the path to growth and healing.

What you will find in the pages of this book is a toolbox that will help you craft the skills you need to improve your mental health and the quality of your daily functioning. I am going to show you just some of the ways that you can actively cope with, heal from, and eventually rise above your anxiety in a meaningful and long-lasting way. I am going to introduce small, yet practical ways that you can improve your stress management strategies and begin the path to good mental health. I encourage you to make the most of this opportunity and to dive into what you are about to learn with excitement and focus. Enjoy the journey!

Chapter 1:

Worry Nut: Anxiety in a Nutshell

Before you can get to building your tailor-made stress and anxiety management strategies, you need to understand what anxiety is and what brings it about. In this chapter, I am going to give you a brief breakdown of how your mind and body respond to anxiety and why they both respond as they do. Next, we are going to look at how to use physical tension and movement to identify your anxiety and how you can use both of these to improve your performance. Finally, we will delve into recognizing the red flags in your mental health so that you can seek professional help. In this section, we're going to cover a few therapy styles that are especially helpful for dealing with anxiety.

That Anxious Feeling: Exploring Anxiety as a Normal Emotion

We've touched on the various physical sensations that you can experience when you are anxious about something. I think we can agree that anxiety is an unpleasant and often uncomfortable emotion. It is also a normal human emotion that serves a purpose. At normal levels, anxiety can and is meant to help us exercise caution and easily identify the best ways to keep ourselves safe. When you are faced with a stressful situation, perhaps a looming deadline or having to make an important decision that could affect your future in a major way, you will feel anxious because you are worried about how things will turn out. But the feeling usually goes away during the performance of the task, and by time you are done with what you had to do, your emotions have gone back to equilibrium. Your mind and your body signal to each other that you've come out unscathed at best, and, at worst, you've learned how to navigate similar situations in the future. For most of us, we don't think about how to deal with that feeling after it's passed because it is so unpleasant. Unfortunately, your desire to avoid the emotional and cognitive part of anxiety means that you do not teach yourself how to deal with it. Instead, you sort of just let the emotion wash over you and drift you about until it passes.

Life in our modern times is such that you are bound to go through every day under some sort of stress. When you are exposed to stress triggers (known as stressors) every day without learning how to effectively manage your stress, you will develop anxiety. Anxiety can be characterized as a fear of some vague, future threat, and the more you feel that you have no control over any given circumstance or its anticipated outcome, the higher your anxiety levels will be. An example of an anxiety-inducing situation that is common to many young people is having to choose a career. Maybe you are still in the early stages of trying to figure out what your interests are and how you can turn those interests into skills that you can make money from or you are in the later stages where you've figured all that out and now you need to take some sort of action and commit to your decision. Whatever the case may be, you may find yourself very anxious because you want to make sure that you have accounted for all the possible outcomes of your decision and made contingency plans where necessary, while simultaneously being overwhelmed by the thought of having to actually live through those moments and facing the actual outcomes. As a result, you can find yourself in one of two situations: the first being that you become obsessed with thinking about all the worst possible outcomes, even the most unlikely ones, and convincing yourself that you will definitely end up in one of those outcomes. This increases your fears and if it continues for a long time, you will end up being convinced that you cannot handle whatever problems you may encounter, which further feeds your anxiety. It is a vicious cycle that can be hard to break from. In the second possible scenario, you could become so overwhelmed by the fear of the unknown that you find yourself unable to take any action because the fear has essentially paralyzed you into inactivity.

Of course, there is a reason why your body reacts this way, and we are going to look into those reasons and how you can use your body's natural response to stress and anxiety to your advantage.

Heart in Motion: The Role/Physiology of the Anxiety Response

We briefly touched on what anxiety can feel like in the body in the introduction, but where do these sensations come from? What actually happens to you on a physiological level? And why does it happen?

When you're under a considerable amount of stress, your mind believes that you're exposed to some sort of impending threat, and it alerts your body that there might be a need to get up and defend itself. It could be a real threat, or it could be something you perceive to be threatening simply because of your uncertainty or because you're worried about a lack of control in a foreign situation. Because your brain cannot tell the difference between a real threat and a perceived one, the body's stress response is the same in both instances. It goes without saying that the stress response is very useful when you're a real attack but can wreak havoc in your body if it was deployed unnecessarily. This response starts with your brain and makes its way across your body.

Our stress response was developed in prehistoric times when we lived in the wild and were exposed to all manner of physical threats to our safety. For the most part, whatever threats humans were faced with back then required some sort of physical movement on their part. Maybe they had to wrestle a lion or run away from a herd of buffalo that were about to trample them. The problem is that our stress response has not evolved since its development in prehistoric man, so when you are anxious about something and your mind detects that threatened state, it still triggers your body to release the same hormones that are meant to help your body prepare to physically respond to the threat. Two of the most important hormones to know here are adrenaline and cortisol, which give us a burst of energy and sharpened focus and actively place the body in its stress response (which is commonly known as the fight-or-flight response). As the name suggests, this physiological response will make you either want to run for your life or stay and fight.

Without getting into the scientific nitty-gritty, what you need to know is that when you are in fight-or-flight mode, your body prioritizes the functions you would need to survive in a life-threatening situation.

That's why you may find that you don't really have much of an appetite when you are anxious, because your body figures that you don't need to be eating when you are fighting or running for your life.

Some of the typical physiological changes include a spike in your blood pressure and heart rate, which makes you breathe faster so that your bloodstream can send nutrients and oxygen to your muscles much quicker than usual. Your lungs also open up more, allowing you to breathe more deeply and be able to hold your breath longer if necessary. Because your blood is being redirected to the essential functions only, you may find yourself looking a bit paler than usual or having cold and clammy hands and feet. Your pupils will dilate, allowing you to see better. You may also find yourself feeling a bit more tension in your body because your muscles are being pumped with all these extra nutrients and are ready to spring into action (*Understanding the Stress Response*, 2020).

There is a third, lesser-known response when you're in stress mode called the freeze response. Although it serves a similar purpose to the fight-or-flight response, it causes a drop in your heart rate and encourages you to take a moment to gather your senses and calculate which moves are less likely to remove you from danger. When your body is in freeze mode, your vision improves so that you can scout the area and get a better understanding of your surroundings. Experts have suggested that the freeze response is related to our tendency to catastrophize and disassociate in stressful or traumatic moments (West, 2021).

As you can see, our stress response is tailor-made to get us out of a state of rest and jolt us into action. But the trouble is that nowadays, the average person is not faced with life-threatening situations as often as prehistoric man was. Our society has developed in a way that almost guarantees our physical safety. Of course, there are exceptions to the level of physical safety you can expect depending on factors such as your lifestyle, geographical location, and so on. However, most modern stressors are psychological, financial, or social in nature, and are not really threats to your wellbeing *per se*. For example, you may be stressed about meeting a certain target at school or at work, but even if you don't meet your target, you can simply try again at the next available opportunity. Sure, it may momentarily feel like your life will be ruined if you don't perform as expected, but the reality is that you can always try again or maybe even try your hand at something different.

The challenge for you as a modern human is learning how to identify your personal threshold for anxiety—the level at which you can still perform your tasks without being overwhelmed by the anxiety—and understanding how to harness that energy for your benefit. Allowing your body to spend long periods in the fight-or-flight mode can have devastating long-term effects on your health. If you have chronic stress, you're more likely to experience permanent memory impairment, heart disease, high blood pressure, and weight problems. Under normal circumstances, the stress response is able to regulate itself and have your bodily functions go back to normal once the stressor has been addressed. But if you are constantly under stress or feeling anxious, you risk weakening the normal functioning of your respiratory, cardio-vascular, and nervous systems (*Understanding the Stress Response*, 2020).

However, if you learn how to bring your body in and out of its stress response at will, you'll get to monopolize the benefits of the stress response with minimal interaction with its negative side effects. To do that, you need to understand how stress and anxiety can be used as a tool to sharpen your problem-solving skills, improve your focus, and enhance your overall performance in any sphere of your life.

Tension, Movement, and Performance: The Lesser-Known Roles of Anxiety in Our Lives.

From what we learned above, you should now understand why tension is one of the natural responses to emotional or physical stress. When your mind senses danger, it tells your muscles to contract as they brace themselves for you to literally move yourself out of harm's way. This tension and contraction usually occurs in the neck, limbs, and chest, as that is where the brain commonly sends signals to (Gillman, 2017). If you think about it, these are the areas that would be engaged if you were to run or fight. However, other areas may also be affected. For example, you might find that when you're anxious you suddenly have a stomach ache or you feel nauseous. During prehistoric times, people were still figuring out what was safe to eat and food could be scarce from time to time. So, if your body thought you'd eaten something poisonous, it would make you feel nauseous so that you'd get rid of what you'd just consumed. Likewise, if you were suddenly forced to flee into an area that seemed dry with no animals to hunt for food, your mind would suppress your appetite so that you could have enough time to look for food (Horn, 2007).

If you are constantly anxious and you don't find ways to release the tension in your muscles, it will increase as time goes by. Eventually, this tension can lead to actual physical pain that can have long-lasting effects on your body if it's not released. A lot of people often find themselves trapped in a vicious cycle of experiencing muscular pain caused by anxiety and only looking for ways to numb their feeling of it instead of looking to release the tension in their bodies or dealing with the source of anxiety. They find it hard to break the cycle of pain and anxiety because they may be so overwhelmed by the anxiety that they medicate the pain away instead of developing sustainable pain relief strategies as step one of healthily dealing with the anxiety.

One of the best and easiest ways to tackle anxiety is through exercise. This is especially helpful when you are in the thick of fight-or-flight mode and you need a way to regulate your emotions and bring calm into the body. It's important to note that you don't have to partake in strenuous or high-impact exercises to combat the effects of the stress response. Exercise can be intimidating to some people, and so it's important to state from the onset that we're not talking about running a marathon or lifting weights. Even taking a short walk, dancing, or washing the car can help. The idea is simply to get your mind out of its overstimulated mental space and have it focus on something else. When you move your body, that tension that's been building in your muscles is slowly released and the physical pain you usually experience when you are overly stressed is alleviated. We've seen how the stress response is developed to get your body out of its state of rest and into action, so why not listen to your body? Instead of fidgeting and having to deal with aches and cramps on top of already being mentally overwhelmed, you can kill two birds with one stone by simply moving your body a little.

There are a number of ways to get the body moving and the mind relaxing. Whatever you choose to do, it helps if you choose a task or exercise that requires you to be focused instead of zoned out and stuck in your stressed mind. For some people, taking mindful walks or runs is the right remedy. They focus on the sensations and sounds around them like chirping birds, car horns, the feel of the wind on their skin, and so on. For others, they need to do something that forces them out of their minds or else they will drift right back into it without even being aware. So, these people would rather do tasks that require precision, like woodwork or cooking a new meal from a recipe book.

When you bring yourself into reality, it's easier for you to rationalize through what is making you anxious and objectively come up with practical solutions to your problems. This is also a great way to deal with a tendency to catastrophize and get stuck on the worst possible outcomes, even those that are far removed from reality. People who catastrophize get to a point where they can't differentiate outlandish exaggerations of their mind from negative outcomes that are possible. To them, being afraid to go out into the rain because they don't want to get wet and because they're afraid of getting struck by lightning are equally possible.

Part of the reason why physical exercise is a great way to decrease physical tension is because it releases these feel-good hormones called endorphins in the body. Endorphins are natural pain killers that also reduce stress and improve your mood. So, if you want to maximize tension release, you should find a hobby that requires a bit of movement from you. Maybe you can take up golf or finally sign up for those dance classes you've been thinking about.

Moreover, teaching yourself to do a bit of physical exercise or movement when you find yourself overwhelmed by stress can help you find your anxiety threshold. This is the breaking point between "healthy" anxiety and a disordered response to it. It's the point where you can be anxious and still perform your daily tasks or have the ability to tackle whichever threat or fear triggered the anxiety in the first place. Because the fight-or-flight response makes you more focused and energized, you will perform better than normal when you learn how to take yourself from being overstimulated and overwhelmed to using the stress as a motivator. It's like we said earlier: You cannot completely remove the fear of the unknown from your life, but you can learn how to harness it to work in your favor. It is a trial-and-error process that will require you to observe what your stress triggers are, whether you are able to recognize when you are stressed, and how you naturally react to stress. Once you've identified all these factors, you'll be able to sit down and come up with effective stress-coping mechanisms that feel natural and right for you.

It might seem like there are a lot of factors at play here, but I want you to appreciate that what we're learning here is how to make gradual changes to our maladaptive coping mechanisms. All this information is here so that you can understand anxiety from every possible angle. The reason it's so difficult to get a handle on your anxiety without the proper skills is exactly because it is a multi-faceted emotion that operates on both the mind and the body. Effective coping mechanisms need to be able to tackle anxiety at its root, and you're more likely to stick with something that feels counterintuitive if you understand why it operates the way it does.

Identifying Mental Health "Red Flags" and Seeking Help

Like everything in life, anxiety is a double-edged sword. On the one hand, you can use your anxiety to your benefit if you know to identify and curb it before it moves past your personal threshold. On the other hand, it can take over your life if you don't learn how to manage it. If you're constantly exposed to stressors and you're having an increasingly hard time managing it, you're at risk to develop a disordered response to stress as anxiety. There are a number of anxiety disorders that you may suffer from as time goes on. These include:

- generalized anxiety disorder

- social anxiety disorder

- selective mutism

- panic disorder

- substance-induced anxiety disorder

- specific phobias (agoraphobia, claustrophobia, etc.)

When your fears get to the point that they hinder your ability to perform daily tasks because you're simply too overwhelmed to function, your anxieties might be developed to the point that they need you to seek professional help. Of course, there are some mental health disorders that have a genetic component, meaning that you're more likely to suffer from that specified disorder because it runs in your family. For example, a study found that generalized anxiety disorder has a heritability of about 30% (Gottschalk & Domschke, 2017). So, if someone in your family suffered from generalized anxiety disorder, then there's a 30% chance of you suffering from it too. But whether you're genetically predisposed or not, having maladaptive and ineffective coping mechanisms makes it easier for your anxiety to get out of hand. If you're concerned about the severity of your anxiety, then it's a good idea to do some research and find a licensed therapist that can put you on a therapy-based treatment plan.

There are a number of different therapeutic styles available to you. We're going to look at some of the styles that have been shown to be the most effective in treating anxiety.

Cognitive Behavior Therapy

Cognitive behavior therapy (CBT) is the most common form of talk therapy for anxiety disorders. CBT seeks to understand the link between your thoughts and emotions, how your body responds to those thoughts and emotions, and how your actions/behaviors are influenced by all these factors. Under CBT, the therapist helps you address your anxiety at each of these levels with the hope that you can eventually develop a personalized set of stress-management skills that you can apply in your life without the encouragement of a therapist.

The CBT treatment plan is based on a few core concepts that inform how the treatment is carried out. One of the most important core concepts for CBT practitioners is the idea that a person's psychological problems are caused by ineffective thinking patterns and learned behavioral patterns that are equally ineffective. The practitioners believe that you can learn how to cope with your psychological problems in ways that relieve the symptoms of anxiety and allow you to function at your best. The more you implement the new thinking patterns and behavior you learn during your treatment, the better your anxiety will become until your responses are no longer disordered. CBT treatment teaches you practices like how to confront your fears and deactivate your body's stress response by intentionally calming your mind and bringing your body back to a relaxed state.

CBT is a talk-based therapy, so a typical CBT session involves your therapist asking you to explain a problem or stress trigger that you are currently struggling with. The therapist will then ask you how you think and feel about the situation and how your body has responded to this stressor. You will then work through breaking down your distorted thinking patterns on the problem and reevaluating the problem in a more realistic way. One of the differences between CBT and other therapeutic styles is its focus on dealing with your stress in the present. It does not give much focus to factors such as family history, past traumas, and other things that may have caused your anxiety disorder. CBT's talk-based methodology means that you only have one-on-one talk sessions and occasional assignments to complete in your own space; there are no other treatment methods involved. This is done so that the therapist can see whether you are able to implement the skills and tools you've learnt on your own without reverting back to your old responses. CBT is a great therapy option if you're not comfortable with group sessions and having to work with multiple therapists.

Dialectical Behavior Therapy

Dialectical behavior therapy (DBT) is an adapted form of cognitive behavioral therapy. Its methodology is specifically reworked to focus on people who are intensely aware of their feelings and have a hard time regulating those feelings. The people who are ideal candidates for DBT have usually begun taking part in self-destructive behaviors such as drinking, substance abuse, and disordered eating as a way to numb or distract themselves from their intense emotions. DBT focuses its treatment plan on helping you understand your emotions and giving you the skills to face them head on so that you engage with them constructively. Once you learn how to do that, you're able to make positive changes in your life by abandoning your self-destructive behaviors and creating boundaries for yourself to keep from relapsing.

The driving philosophy behind DBT can be found in the word "dialectical." Oxford Languages (n.d) defines "dialectical" as something that is concerned with or acts through opposing forces. Likewise, DBT acknowledges that life is complex and often requires us to learn that two things that seem to be opposites of each other can be true at the same time and coexist within the same space. For example, you could be a person that is self-confident but doubts their self-worth in specific circumstances. Our responsibility, then, is to find a balance between these opposing beliefs and learn how to manage the negative and difficult feelings that come with these opposite states of being so that they do not control our lives.

The DBT treatment finds its basis in the following five key functions:

1. The first function is to improve the individual's life skills. Because people undergoing this treatment struggle with emotional regulation, the treatment aims to help them develop new and effective methods for emotional regulation, particularly in stressful or triggering environments. The goal is to teach them how to navigate these situations in a way that builds healthy interpersonal relationships and does not lead to a heightening of the situation.

2. The second function deals with successfully applying the skills the person has learnt in real time in their personal lives and in various environments. For this to be monitored, they will be given homework assignments to practice these skills and figure out how they can be adapted to your current lifestyle so that it's easier for you to implement them.

3. The third function focuses on the person's destructive behaviors (eating disorders, self-harm, etc.). During the one-on-one talk sessions with the client, the therapist will have them complete some sort of self-monitoring form to see how often they have engaged in their identified harmful behaviors. The person is given strategies to implement whenever they feel like

indulging in harmful behaviors. Additionally, the therapist helps the person investigate and understand the causes of these behaviors. Once the therapist and client understand where the destructive behaviors stem from and what maintains them, it becomes easier for them to develop methods that will get the client motivated to root out the destructive behaviors and keep them motivated about making these changes, even during triggering circumstances. Importantly, the program allows for the client to call their therapist when they feel themselves being tempted to numb themselves with their behavior of choice. The therapist will then walk the client through the progress they've made thus far and help them move past the temptation in real time.

4. The next function focuses on restructuring the client's environment in a way that supports their changed behavior and makes it difficult for them to fall back into those behaviors. This may require the client to get a new social circle, create boundaries with the friends and family that enable these behaviors, or move to a new environment entirely. The therapists are closely involved in this function to ensure that the changes required do not overwhelm the client and cause them to relapse into their previous behaviors. This is one of the harder functions of the program because it involves people other than the client. Some of these people may not respond well to boundaries and a renegotiation of their relationship with the client, so they may lash out and try to sabotage the client's progress or ostracize them.

5. The last function relates to the therapists themselves. Because the individuals who undergo DBT treatment often have a lot of destructive behaviors that are enmeshed and need to be removed, it is typical for the therapists themselves to find themselves demotivated or lacking in the skills to deal with a particular situation. To combat this, the treatment also includes systems of support and feedback from other professionals, emotional validation for the therapist, and continuous skills development. All of this is done in a highly controlled and professional manner to ensure that the clients don't feel that

their private information could be discussed with people they aren't comfortable with.

The intense and involved nature of DBT means that effective treatment requires different settings that support the implementation of each of its functions. A typical DBT treatment plan includes sessions that take place in a group setting, one-on-one talk therapy sessions, and even sessions held over the phone. Dealing with highly emotionally charged people requires a lot of support and a sense of community. The group sessions help the clients to connect with people that know what it is to deal with emotional dysregulation and in this way, they're able to more comfortably lean on each other, share their journeys with ease, and even advise each other on dealing with certain complex situations.

DBT teaches skills such as mindfulness (focusing on the now and centering your senses to the present moment), developing assertiveness, and healthy communication skills in relationships. When an emotionally sensitive person learns how to pull themselves out of an emotionally charged mental space, they're able to reasonably assess their environment, adapt their behavior accordingly and then assert this adaptation to the people around them. A lot of emotionally sensitive people tend to keep their true feelings and opinions to themselves because they want to avoid conflict. This lands them in a lot of uncomfortable and undesirable circumstances that make their dysregulation worse. So, when they learn how to assert themselves, they also need to learn how to healthily communicate this change to others.

As mentioned above, people who are best served by DBT often have a lot of unhealthy behaviors that need to be dealt with methodically. As such, the treatment plan is divided into four stages. In the beginning, the therapist will identify the person's most destructive behaviors and work toward resolving these first. These usually are those behaviors that make the person a danger to themselves, such as suicidal ideas and self-harm tendencies. Once these are addressed, the treatment moves on to the issues that affect the person's quality of life. These include learning how to tolerate distress in the moment and managing their intense emotions. Next, the therapist and the client will work on rebuilding the client's self-confidence and how they engage with their friends and family. The client usually feels shame for their intense emotions and how they choose to soothe themselves before learning positive emotional regulation skills. As such, their sense of worth and how they engage with the world is colored through that lens of shame. They may even have certain relationships that have enabled their self-destructive behaviors that will need to be redefined or completely let go of. Lastly, the treatment's focus shifts toward helping the people live their lives to the fullest as renewed beings who can deal with the world in a healthy way and have the confidence to pursue their goals and dreams.

Internal Family Systems Therapy

Internal family systems therapy (IFS) is a form of talk therapy that is based on the following core belief: Each person has a core Self that has self-esteem and confidence and is whole. Surrounding the core Self are a person's sub-personalities or "parts." These parts hold our traumas and emotions like shame, fear, and anger. Our parts are what form when our minds try to suppress unpleasant experiences by protecting us from harm and controlling the outcomes of unknown and threatening events. These parts are often in conflict with each other and with our core Self, and they interact as family members do—separate but a part of the same root.

Dr. Richard Swartz, the creator of the IFS model, was inspired to create it when he realized that most of his patients would often refer to different "parts" of themselves influencing their behavior and their general outlook on life and the challenges they faced (*Internal Family Systems Therapy*, n.d). For example, someone would tell him about a promotion they had received at work and would go on about how excited they were about the opportunity and how hard they had worked to position themselves as the right person for the job. But then they would mention how a part of them felt that they were underqualified to properly do the job and how that part worried that they would be exposed as a fraud and shamed for being incapable of performing as expected.

According to the IFS model, our parts split themselves into three distinct groups:

1. The Managers - These parts serve to protect us by trying to control our environments and emotions and how we complete daily tasks. Their goal is to have us be as prepared for unknown threats as possible and to control the outcome of these unknown circumstances as much as possible.

2. The Exiles - These parts hold all our trauma and the heavy and often painful memories and emotions that come with the trauma. These parts are exiled into the subconscious by the managers as a way to help us avoid reliving or confronting our emotional distress.

3. The Firefighters - These parts are the bodyguards of the conscious mind. When the exiled parts produce overwhelming and painful emotions that burst through from the subconscious, the firefighters come to the forefront. They try to stop us from feeling the full brunt of those emotions by making us indulge in behaviors that will numb the pain. These may include emotional eating, substance use, or engaging in other risky, yet seemingly exciting behaviors.

On the other end, we find the undamaged core Self. This is who you are in your essence: the trauma-free and whole part of yourself that would be presented to the world had it not been for all the pain, suffering, and trauma you experienced. The IFS model states that the core Self can be identified by the eight Cs and the five Ps. These are:

- Calmness

- Curiosity

- Connectedness

- Confidence

- Courage

- Compassion

- Clarity

- Creativity

- Playfulness

- Presence

- Persistence

- Patience

- Perspective

The goal of IFS is to help you heal and transform your parts to be in alignment with your core Self so that there is harmony within your being. The treatment achieves this by first helping you identify which parts of your being play which roles in the internal family you have created. Once you've labeled your parts, you and your therapist will pick one part to focus on and begin working on harmonizing it with the core Self. You will then flesh out the isolated part by describing how it functions and how you've experienced it in your life. You will also explore how you feel about this part and how it makes you feel when it comes to the fore in your behaviors and interactions with the world. The next step includes working toward understanding and accepting this part of yourself so that you no longer have any strong emotions toward it, but you simply accept it as a part of yourself. The final step is to confront the fears of this particular part of yourself and examine what it would mean if you were to bring it into alignment with the soft and untainted core Self.

IFS treatment requires a lot of self-reflection and introspection. You will be required to be honest and vulnerable with yourself and to keep track of how you react to different triggers in the world and within your particular environment.

Reality Therapy

Reality therapy is a type of talk therapy that aims to change the person's worldview and help them manage life's challenges in a constructive way. Reality therapy is similar to CBT in that the treatment focuses on the present and teaches you how to manage your emotions and effectively deal with emotions and stressors.

This treatment is based on Choice Theory, which states that humans have five basic needs and their behaviors are all aimed at having those needs fulfilled. These basic needs are survival, power, freedom, fun, and love or a sense of belonging. According to Choice Theory, love or a sense of belonging is the strongest of the basic needs because it offers us community, support, and protection. Practitioners of this theory believe that all our behaviors are a result of choices that we make in order to fulfill one or more of our basic needs (*Choice Theory*, 2019).

Humans instinctively know that the easiest way to have our basic needs met is by cultivating caring and authentic relationships with the people in our communities. However, this requires us to be vulnerable with ourselves and others, forcing us to face our own darkness and possibly being seen as different by the very people we seek to build relations with and being ostracized. So, instead, we choose to threaten, manipulate, and belittle others into submission of our will, somehow believing that this will create the camaraderie and protection we desire. But the true outcome of this is fractured, disingenuous relationships that are fraught with resentment, anger, and frustration. This creates a toxic cycle of inauthentic and harmful interactions and behaviors that can cause serious mental health issues if they are not addressed and broken.

Reality therapy can be especially challenging because it forces the client to shed their socialized mask and show up as their truest, most vulnerable self. We're all socialized to act or think a certain way from our very first day on this planet, so ripping that mask off can be a very slow and painful process. The client has to confront every bad decision and every selfish move they've ever made that informs their current behavior. The therapist and client focus on developing the client's sense of self and self-control, and a lot of emphasis is placed on taking responsibility for the behaviors they have chosen to partake in as part of their desire to have their needs met. Here, the client is encouraged to take responsibility for their past destructive and toxic behaviors and choose to behave in ways that will help them authentically connect with others. Most people find it difficult to accept that they've caused harm to others or themselves because they were too afraid to be vulnerable and real. Therapists who practice reality therapy often have to deal with intense denial from their clients and may have to guide some clients through an identity crisis.

However, it is important to note that this therapeutic style has been criticized by many people, primarily because it rejects the notion that some behaviors are the result of mental illnesses because Choice Theory sees all behaviors as choices that a person actively makes. As a direct result of this view, practitioners of Choice Therapy are often against the use of medication to treat mental illnesses and many have criticized reality therapy's dismissal of the power that our subconscious has on us and its effect on how we behave and engage with the world, particularly in stressful or uncertain circumstances that induce an overwhelming amount of anxiety within us.

Gestalt Therapy

Gestalt therapy is similar to CBT in that it also focuses on increasing your awareness and presence in the moment rather than excessively delving into your past experiences to help treat your anxiety. In this therapy treatment, you are taught that your thoughts, emotions, and behaviors are influenced by your present environment. The word "gestalt" is a German word that can be loosely understood to mean "whole." This word sums up the ideology behind this treatment: No one experience, trait, or emotion can define a person. Instead, every person is understood to be complex and ever-growing in an ever-changing environment.

As part of its goal to increase your sense of awareness and your ability to self-direct at any moment, Gestalt therapy teaches you how to accept and trust what you feel at any given moment instead of relying on what you may have felt in the past during the same or a similar experience. You are guided to approach these feelings with empathy and open-mindedness instead of judgment and annoyance.

In a typical Gestalt therapy session, the therapist tries to draw you into the present or get you to express what you felt and thought during a particular experience by having you do intellectual or physical exercises such as re-enacting certain moments, role-play, or asking you to draw out those moments. The therapist's goal during these exercises is to help you bring those experiences to life within the therapeutic setting so that they can ask you what is happening in that moment and how you feel about it. During these exercises, you learn how to be aware of your thoughts and behaviors so that you can examine and understand them. This is particularly important for people suffering from anxiety because we often find ourselves unable to remember certain moments, much less how we felt during those moments. Our minds are often so preoccupied with just trying to get us through whatever is happening that we barely take the time to be present and aware because we are functioning on the memories of the past to get us through the present.

In the long run, continual use of these exercises not only helps with your self-awareness; they also help you accept your past experiences for what they were and make peace with their outcomes, increase your ability to deal with stressful situations, and make you an overall more responsible person because you are able to own your mistakes and past poor behaviors without judgment or blame. All of this makes you a more confident person because you learn to accept yourself as a whole and complex being who is both flawed and wonderful. You no longer spend your energy resisting yourself and the present, and this allows you to spend that energy cultivating better ways to handle stressful situations and healthier methods to have your needs met.

As with all "here and now" focused therapy styles, the downside is that the treatment plan does not cater to understanding your past experiences and how they have shaped you, nor does it look at hereditary behaviors.

There Is No Shame in Seeking Help

Anxiety has become one of the leading mental health challenges in the world, with an alarmingly high number of people admitting to struggling with debilitating anxiety on a daily basis. This is especially true for teenagers and young adults who are having to face the most uncertain times of their lives in a world that is rapidly changing in unpredictable ways in almost every sphere of life. It then makes sense that anxiety, which notoriously thrives on the fear of the unknown, currently has the world in a chokehold.

As you grow older, you move from being in environments where people generally tell you how to think, feel, and behave to a space where you have to self-direct for the first time with little to no guidance or understanding of what it is to move in the world without a guiding hand on your back. You find yourself faced with complex situations, some of which you never knew could exist, much less that you would encounter them and have to overcome them. It is during these times that you may find yourself needing guidance and support, particularly as it relates to your mental health. But you may find yourself ashamed to admit that you need that kind of help because it seems like everyone else has a handle on things and you don't want to embarrass yourself by admitting to people that you are struggling a little. Or perhaps when you do have the courage to speak up, no one seems to understand or they ridicule you for expressing yourself. So, you resign yourself to struggling in silence.

Feeling helpless when you are overwhelmed by anxiety is a common response. So is developing self-destructive behaviors that numb you from the intensity of your feelings and seem to get you through the days ahead. But you know that there has to be a better way to live your life.

Mental health is a spectrum, with good mental health practices and diagnoses on the one end and more complex and destructive ones on the other. The good thing about it is that you can always reverse, or at least learn to manage, any harm that your mental health has suffered with the right strategies and support. The bad news is that if you leave mental health issues unresolved, they build on one another and become complicated and multi-layered. The longer you leave these issues unattended, the more effort it will take from your part to understand and resolve them. It's good to seek help as soon as you start identifying patterns of disordered behavior from yourself.

Our minds are our most powerful tools. What we perceive to be real, how we feel about what we see and experience, how we think and process the world around us, all those things are controlled by our minds. So, it's important that we take all the necessary steps to improve our mental health. When used correctly, our mind is our greatest weapon. But if we let the mind run rampant, it can easily become our strongest opponent.

There is no shame in seeking help, finding healthy coping mechanisms, and building a community of support and understanding for yourself. It is okay to acknowledge that you may be in a period of your life where the circumstances before you are beyond your current capabilities and you need someone who will guide you through them and help you build healthy ways to handle your emotions and curate productive behaviors. Allow yourself the grace to admit that you will never know everything, and that extends to dealing with parts of yourself.

Chapter 2:

Stems and Roots: Sources of

Anxiety in the Modern World

A lot of things can make us anxious, especially in an ever-changing modern world that sees new developments at breakneck speed. These developments have improved the way we communicate, made difficult tasks easier to complete or delegate, and have generally improved our quality of life in all spheres. However, they have also made it easier for us to be held against a microscope and scrutinized by others for every fault and flaw. The rise of social media has made it easier for people to stalk and harass others, while the apps we use for convenience are simultaneously collecting data on our behaviors and using that information for the benefit of their financial bottom line.

While we cannot control some of these things and how they affect us, there are still areas of our lives that we have complete control over. An essential part of creating the best stress management strategies for our mental health is exploring our unique situations and creating solutions that are tailor-made to the problems we've identified. In this chapter, we're going to explore some of the common causes of anxiety in the modern world.

The Price of Knowing More and Not Knowing More

The modern world thrives on the idea of a global community. Every advancement that is made seems to be geared toward bringing the world together under one umbrella and creating ways for us to understand and learn from each other. You can now watch a historic event from thousands of miles away at the click of a button. But the more we know about what is happening around us, the easier it is for us to recognize potential threats. These threats, whether right at our doorstep or across the globe, can elicit some form of anxiety from us. You could be watching a news report on the economic status of a country that is continents away from your own and suddenly find yourself worried about your own country's economics and how they affect your personal finances. What started as an evening catching up on world events could very easily end with you stuck in a catastrophizing loop.

Humans crave information because it helps us learn and adapt to foreign environments, and it helps us feel like we have some semblance of control over our lives and our futures. But what happens when that information does more harm than good? How do we filter through the information storm and focus on news that is beneficial to us?

You might think that completely disengaging from the information storm is a great way to avoid being overwhelmed by knowledge of countless real and perceived threats. But not knowing what can happen next is an equally strong source of anxiety. If humans crave information because it gives them a sense of certainty and control, then completely depriving yourself of that information is not an adaptive and productive solution to the problem. People cannot survive for long in an unpredictable environment. We are wired to learn and adapt to our environments to maximize our safety and the use of our resources. If we're in environments that don't allow us to adequately adapt and apply our newfound knowledge to our advantage, we run the risk of destroying both ourselves and the environment. When humans are overwhelmed and dysregulated, they cannot logically process and understand what is happening around them. Not only do they fail to learn and adapt as necessary, they also tend to indulge in destructive and unhealthy behaviors that negatively impact them and everything around them.

When the body does not have the chance to catch up to its surroundings and feel some sort of stability, it's constantly under strain because it never has a chance to have its functions synchronized with each other and the environment. This can have long term negative effects on the body's proper functioning, leaving it weakened and unable to protect itself when faced with real threats to its survival.

Our pursuit for knowledge is fraught with pitfalls. If we open ourselves up to knowing as much as possible, we increase our risk of anxiety and stress because we may encounter information that makes us anxious, impeding our ability to function properly. But if we close ourselves off to that information, our fear of uncertainty and lack of control equally makes us anxious because we come to realize that we don't have any means to prepare for the future, and we're left feeling helpless and exposed.

The Problem With Anticipation

Fritz Perls was a renowned German psychiatrist who dedicated his life to understanding the functions of the human mind and what influences our behaviors. He was well-known for his work on awareness and even founded a therapeutic style that focuses on expanding a person's awareness of the interconnectivity of the senses, behaviors, and the environment (Gestalt Theory, n.d).

Perls believed that the main reason we are anxious is because we keep on anticipating threats. As a proponent of living in and being wholly aware of one's present environment, Perls believed that the best way to deal with anxiety is by being aware of yourself as a holistic being so that you can understand how your environment affects you. When you are always anticipating what the future has in store, you are never present and alert within your current environment, and so it becomes difficult for you to be self-directed. When your focus is on the externals, your behavior and your response to the environment is determined by others. You don't have the chance to take a beat and intentionally redirect your behavior and responses because you act on impulse. And sometimes, your impulsives may have greatly miscalculated the threat of danger or misread the circumstances. Unfortunately, by the time you realize that this is the case, you've already made an inappropriate response that has probably made the situation worse or put you in real harm's way.

It is normal to wonder about the future and to have a desire to be prepared for it, but constant anticipation has debilitating effects on your mental health, particularly if your focus is on the possible negative outcomes, which is often the case. If you train your mind to center itself at times of crises, you're more likely to handle whatever is causing your anxiety in a logical and calm manner.

The Irony of Modern Connection

We've touched on how social media and the Internet have allowed us to connect with millions of people from across the globe at the touch of a button. But the trouble with this is that a lot of people have opted to replace normal face-to-face relationships with the people around them with the connections they make online. Our generation has become lonelier than ever, with people turning to social media as their only form of connection with others. The truth is that these online connections are often not as secure as the attachments you create in real life because they are usually based on just one aspect of who you are and cannot be relied on for support at all times.

People are social beings, and all of our most basic human needs rely on secure human relationships for them to be satisfactorily met. Having people to interact, laugh, and share life with can boost our sense of worth and love and reduce our exposure to stress and anxiety. Having real-life relationships with people makes it easier to grow an organic and authentic bond with others that can withstand the trials and tribulations of life. When you're experiencing a hard time in life, you want someone who will be there to listen, give a warm hug, and reassure you that everything is going to work out. Just having that physical sense of support, security, and love can do wonders for your self-confidence and make it easier for you to take on your problems.

The problem with social media connections is that they cannot provide you with a fulfilling and real sense of community. No matter how close your online community is, there are some aspects that it simply will not be able to fill, be it because of distance, cultural differences, or a lack of understanding of your needs. And for the most part, social media connections begin with people trying to impress or being impressed by one another. The basis of a lot of these connections is therefore competitive and not genuine. When you're experiencing a challenge in your life, you're less likely to reach out for help from a person that you want to perceive you in a certain light. You'd rather suffer in silence than let that person see you as weaker than them or incapable of dealing with life.

Another major problem with social media connections is that people often sacrifice spending time with their friends and family to be online with their virtual community. This weakens your real-life connections because you're no longer making the time to nurture and protect them. All of your time and energy is spent elsewhere, and you have nothing left to give the people around you. If your focus is not on the present and your relationships with your family and friends, you may miss their attempts to try and reconnect with you because you're not paying attention. Sometimes, you may even find yourself getting annoyed at their constant attempts to spend time with you because you have other ideas on how to spend that time. This can create feelings of jealousy and resentment from your loved ones, who feel like that you would rather focus your efforts on spending time with strangers rather than strengthening your relationships with them.

When you're chronically online, you may start to negatively compare your relationships with the relationships of others that you see online and find yourself being put off by their attempts at reconnection with you. Seeing what you think are healthier and more fulfilling relationships can make you seek out similar relationships with other people, leading to betrayal or resentment on your part. Unfortunately, most people only show the good parts of their lives online, and quite a bit of content on there is curated to portray a certain ideal or image that is removed from reality. It can be difficult to remember that though, especially when you feel undervalued or otherwise unsatisfied in your own relationships. You'll begin taking the people around you for granted because they don't fit a newfound ideal that you want to mold them into, forgetting to cherish the good and to be grateful that they love and accept the bad parts of who you are as well.

The Art and Tragedy of Killing Time

The average lifestyle in the modern world is fast-paced, with constant feedback being thrown at us and not enough time given to process it all. When you finally get the chance to be alone and to sit in silence and peace, you can find yourself feeling uncomfortable with this foreign state of being. This is why a lot of people would rather mindlessly pass the time by doing things that aren't of any significance, things that they probably won't even remember the next day.

Being mindful and fully present in the things you do to pass the time can be a daunting task, especially when you've spent a significant part of your life being anxious and overstimulated. Present-centeredness and mindful living require you to confront your fears and get in tune with your inner being, and that's not an enjoyable place to be in when you've been in servitude to those fears for so long. Peace begins to resemble boredom and your mind tries to seek out the chaotic setup it's accustomed to. We are creatures of habit, and we desire certainty and comfort. Rather than using our time wisely, we would rather spend it under constant distraction because it's what we're used to. So we mindlessly scroll through our phones and indulge in self-destructive behaviors that make the time go by faster.

However, even in this ever-chaotic environment that we willfully engage in, we have those rare moments of lucidity when we realize that our lives are out of sorts. Killing time can only work for so long, and no matter how skillful you've become at the art of it, a part of you knows that there's a better way to exist. That part of you will always be aware of all the time wasted on nonsense, all the opportunities you've passed on because you were too afraid to take a chance and bet on yourself.

Your tactics at killing time only work because they thrust you right back into that all too familiar space of being overwhelmed and overstimulated. Ironically, that very same environment is what makes you anxious. So, while you may think that you want an escape from your anxiety because it's exhausting and unhealthy, you may be unwittingly exposing yourself to more anxiety by the ways you choose to kill time.

Being aware of the things that put you in an anxious state is important if you want to successfully break the cycle of anxiety. You need to interrogate the root of some of your behaviors with brutal honesty. The things that are within your control can only remain that way if you're engaging them authentically and holistically.

Chapter 3:

Skills and Strategies: Building Your

Personal Toolkit

Understanding your anxiety is the first and most important part of the journey toward healing your mental health. Now you are ready to enter the next phase: actively combating that anxiety by learning effective stress management skills and building new habits for yourself. In this chapter, we are going to explore some of the skills and strategies you can use to fight anxiety and show you some practical exercises that you can implement in your daily life. By the end of this chapter, you will have a wealth of resources from which you can build your personal anti-anxiety toolkit!

Cognitive Reframing

The first skill we're going to explore and develop is the art of cognitive reframing. How we think about our experiences determines how we feel about them, which in turn affects our behavior and the results of those behaviors. So, if you think negatively about a specific situation, your actions in relation to it will be negative because your feelings about it are negative as well. When you inevitably experience negative outcomes as a result of your own response to the situation, you will reinforce the idea that the situation or experience in itself is, and will always be, negative. You will essentially create a self-fulfilling prophecy about that situation and other similar situations because of how you respond to them.

The opposite is equally true. If your thoughts about a specific experience or situation are positive, you will have positive and productive behaviors toward it because your feelings are positive as well. This means you will likely have a positive outcome to the situation because your reaction to it was to do something productive. You could salvage a potentially bad situation simply by how you respond to it and in doing so, you build your self-confidence by learning that you can tackle and overcome bad experiences, and you slowly teach your mind that certain experiences do not require an anxious meltdown because you have proven to yourself that you can handle it.

People who suffer from anxiety are likely to indulge in a number of negative cognitive distortions. For example, you may find that you tend to focus on the negative aspects of a situation rather than viewing it as a complex matter with both negative and positive aspects. You may also find yourself placing broad generalizations on a number of situations based on one bad experience you had. This can lead you to catastrophize and always expect the worst outcome because you've framed your mind toward the negative.

These cognitive distortions are the unhelpful thoughts that we cling to that make our anxiety worse. When you start confronting, understanding, and reframing these distortions, you minimize their negative effects, and soon these distortions come into your mind less frequently. Cognitive reframing is one of the key skills you learn in CBT, and it's especially helpful if you have social anxiety.

Cognitive reframing is a process and experts have developed steps that you can take to reframe your thoughts. The first being that you need to recognize your automatic thoughts and note what kind of situations trigger those thoughts and if you can identify a pattern there. To do this effectively, it helps if you can write what you have recorded in a journal or something of that nature. Next, you will need to identify the parts of your thoughts that could be distorted toward negativity. For example, maybe you have the generalization that you never fit into any group of people because you are socially awkward or you never know the right thing to say.

The next step is for you to challenge your thoughts by placing them under the microscope of rationality and reason. Ask yourself the following questions: What evidence is there to support this view/conclusion I have made about this situation? Have I taken into account all the complexities of the situation before me? Is my view based on my feelings or on facts? What is the worst that could happen if my thoughts are correct? So, if we apply this to the example we have of someone that is afraid to be in a group of people, the questions that person could ask themselves include the following: Why do I think that I never know the right thing to say in a group of people? Why does there need to be a right thing to say? Why do I automatically think that I will be the outcast in the group when I have not even met the people yet? What would happen if I did end up saying something that doesn't land as I had hoped? What about those times when I found kindred souls within a group of people I had never met before?

Finally, once you have recognized your automatic thoughts and challenged them, you can begin replacing them with positive affirmations and accurate thoughts that are logical and evidence-based. So, in our example, you could replace the negative thought with the following: "I don't need to worry about saying the right thing in unknown social settings because everyone is getting to know each other, same as I am. Sometimes what I say in such situations is well-received and sometimes it's not, but not batting a thousand each time does not make me a socially awkward person. I could be surprised and make a life-long acquaintance or friend in that group or social setting, but the only way I can do that is by being true to myself and being comfortable in who I am, even the unconventional parts of me."

Cognitive reframing can be an intimidating process because it requires you to be present and self-reflective, and that can be difficult to do in circumstances that are emotionally charged or that make you anxious. So, it helps to have tools that will take your mind out of the cluttered and anxious mindset and center in the present. One of the easiest tools is to simply take a few moments to take slow, deep breaths. This helps calm you down because it slows down the pounding heartbeats and regulates your breathing when you find your fight-or-flight response triggered. Once you've calmed yourself down, it's easier for you to ground yourself in the present moment and methodically go through each step of cognitive reframing. Another tip is to mindfully go through the steps of cognitive reframing. This means allowing yourself to focus on being intensely aware of your feelings and thoughts as you immerse yourself in each step. You allow yourself to feel and sense everything around and within you without judging it. Undergoing cognitive reframing in this way instead of flying through the steps so you can get to the end can help you tap into your subconscious and bring up thoughts and feelings that you were not even aware of.

Your anxiety will dramatically improve when you start intentionally engaging with your thoughts, examining them, questioning them, and replacing them with more adaptive and positive ones.

Minimizing Surprise

A major defining factor of anxiety is the immense discomfort with the unknown, or being surprised. Your anxiety is most likely going to peak in spaces and situations where you don't know what to expect so you don't know how to prepare yourself to assimilate into the environment or act in a way that will protect you.

Scientists have done research on how all intelligent, biological life organizes itself and what they found was that all living organisms are biologically wired to minimize surprise, and this is usually done by mimicking learned behavior (Friston, 2009). When you find yourself faced with circumstances where your expectations are subverted and you are left surprised and unprepared, your anxiety spikes. That blank space between your expectations and reality is called free energy.

If your mind continuously fails to make accurate expectations about reality, it's failing to minimize the free energy/surprise that you are exposed to, and that can lead to chronic stress, anxiety, or an anxiety disorder. On the other hand, when your mind has accurately predicted the reality you face, your sense of surprise is minimized and you feel in control. Of course, it's impossible to predict or prepare for future outcomes with 100% certainty, but the goal of minimizing surprise is to bring your levels of stress and anxiety within your personal threshold for them.

There are two commonly used methods to minimize surprise and increase your sense of security and stability in any environment. The first method is by collecting as much data about the anxiety-inducing event as possible. When you are unsure of what to expect from a situation that you have never encountered, the best way to prepare for it is to find out as much as you can about it, possibly from people who have personal experience with the situation. Imagine if you will, the following scenario: You've made a new group of friends and they've invited you to go hiking. You work yourself up into a frenzy in the week leading up to this event because you've never hiked before. You suddenly realize that you're actually afraid of heights, you have no athletic attire, you don't know when last you saw a pair of sneakers in your house, and you're clumsy and could easily fall to your death! This is a typical response for a person that suffers from anxiety. You completely freak out because you're scared to try something new and obsess over everything that could possibly go wrong, and you convince yourself that all these negative (and sometimes unlikely) outcomes will definitely happen to you. Then, when it's time to go on that hiking excursion, you make up some flimsy excuse and bail.

But what if instead of letting your fear of the unknown rule your life, you actually decide that you were going to combat it as much as you can by being prepared. You can ask your friends what they suggest you wear on the trail and then go out and buy the appropriate gear for hiking if you don't have any. Ask them what you need to bring to ensure that you have an enjoyable and safe time with them. Share your concerns and ask them to share their hiking experiences with you.

The second method used to minimize surprise is to expect the worst. This seems to be the easier of the two options, considering that people suffering from anxiety generally tend to have an exaggerated and negative view of the unknown. So, since you are prone to catastrophizing anyway, lean into it, and plan what your reaction will be if all the worst possible outcomes were to actually happen. You don't have the right gear for your hike? You might be a bit uncomfortable, but you'll still be on the trail with your friends and you'll get to the top. You didn't bring any water or snacks with you? Well, your social anxiety may hold you back from asking a friend for a sip of water, but your need to survive will definitely take over and you'll find yourself sharing an energy bar with your friend who may joke about your unpreparedness. You will nonetheless be alive, hydrated, and creating memories.

Whichever method you are most comfortable trying, the end result is the same. You will teach yourself how to deal with uncertainty and increase your resilience in such situations.

Present-Centeredness

Every person that suffers from anxiety has trouble being fully present at any given moment. You can never let yourself enjoy the moment if you're always worried about what your next move will be or what you need to say that will land perfectly with the crowd. When your mind has 1000 different tabs open and each one is vying for your attention as a matter of urgency, it becomes impossible for you to focus on just one thing, much less to focus on the one thing that is in front of you right now. A lot of anxious people subconsciously train themselves to stay in a hyperstimulated mental state even if they are engaged in leisurely activities because it makes it easier for them to just shift their focus from the "fun" activity to thinking about something stressful without missing a beat. I put "fun" in quotation marks there because let's be real: Are you really having a good time if you're only pretending to have fun, while in truth your mind is spinning in a thousand different directions? If you're not fully immersed in the fun experiences, you can't say that you're truly enjoying yourself.

Training your mind to ignore all the distractions that come with being stressed, anxious, or overstimulated takes practice and patience. Learning how to live in the moment not only helps you relieve stress and anxiety, it also increases your productivity and allows you to live a full life with healthier relationships and a deeper sense of self-love.

The most commonly used method in the practice of mindfulness and being present-centered is meditation, but trying to sit in silence with yourself for significant stretches of time can be a daunting and borderline tortuous exercise if your mind is used to being everywhere all at once. You'll likely find yourself wandering back to your million and one anxious thoughts, going through your to-do list for the next day, or relieving your most shameful social faux pas. Instead of setting yourself up for disappointment by taking a bigger first bite of the present-centeredness pie than you can chew, try practicing being present with small things that are already a part of your daily life.

One of the first steps you can take is to challenge yourself to do one thing at a time without trying to complete seven other tasks on the side. For example, you find that you have gotten into the habit of working on a project or finishing homework while listening to music and occasionally scrolling through your phone. Constantly shifting your attention between so many things may be making your anxiety worse, but you don't realize it because you think the background music and phone scrolling are helping to keep you interested or motivated in finishing your task. Of course, multi-tasking is not a bad thing in and of itself. But if you find that you cannot focus on one task at any given time, then you may have gotten so accustomed to being distracted and anxious that you no longer allow yourself to be present even when doing things that bring you joy.

Another useful practice to adopt is teaching yourself to focus on your breathing at any given moment in order to draw you out of autopilot and into the here and now. Breathing is an essential and life-giving function that we do every second without even thinking about it. When you bring yourself to focus on how you are breathing, your mind steps out of its thoughts and your focus shifts to the things around you.

You can kick this practice up a notch by practicing what is known as mindful breathing. This is when you pay attention not only to your breathing, but you expand that focus to other areas of your internal life, such as how your body is feeling, what sounds you are hearing in your body, what your thoughts are, and so on. You can expand your realm of focus as far as you'd like and even try out different deep-breathing styles to feel how your body responds to a change in the flow of breath within.

Tapping into your creativity is another great way to cultivate present-centeredness. Creating space in your day to let your creative juices flow is a great way to help you pay attention to your thoughts and feelings because it requires you to think about what you want to convey or achieve and then focus on executing it the way you see or feel it. This rings true for all creative endeavors, whether it be painting, drawing, journaling, or doing a crafts project. A lot of creatives tap into their emotions to create, so this is also a great way for you to release any suppressed thoughts or feelings that are holding you back from being aligned with your core Self.

If you are a person who enjoys physicality, then perhaps you will be more inclined to partake in exercises that encourage mindful movement and help you feel more connected to your body. These may include Pilates, yoga, and interpretive dance. Any exercise that requires slow and deliberate movement of the body will help you focus on the present.

Of course, there is still meditation as a way to divert your attention to the now. As I mentioned earlier, sitting in silence with your thoughts for a long time can be a scary thing, but who says you need to meditate for an hour for it to be effective? Most people have the impression that you need to sit for a long time and keep your focus exactly where you intended to have it if you want meditation to work for you. The truth is, you can do two-minute sessions and still have a successful meditation session. And it's ok for your mind to wander off now and again, as long as you catch yourself and divert your attention back to where it needs to be. You can sit in silence and simply feel the sensations of your body, or you can focus on a specific mental image or repeat a positive affirmation. There is no right way to meditate, and different things work for different people. You will find that meditating in the morning is what works for some people, while others prefer to do it in the afternoon or in the evening.

The most practical way to begin is to find what works for your lifestyle and your personality. It's a process of trial and error, so don't feel disappointed if it takes you a while to find your meditation groove.

The more you practice redirecting your attention toward the present, the less anxious you become because your focus is no longer on the "what ifs" and is now on the "what is."

Social Media Reset

Humans have a primal, intrinsic need for connection with others. It helps us feel loved, seen, valued, and protected. Social media has helped people connect to hundreds and thousands of people from every corner of the earth, and it can enrich your life and create shared experiences between kindred souls that you would not have met otherwise. Social media has many positive aspects, such as helping people raise awareness on important social and political issues, giving them a platform to express their creativity and share it with the world at little to no cost, and keeping us informed about what happens in the world.

But excessive use of these platforms, especially if used to replace or in disregard of the connections we've made in the real world, can be detrimental not only for the communities we've built over the years but to our mental health as well.

A lot of people find themselves "dead scrolling" through their social media, spending hours scrolling through their phones but having no recollection at the end of what they saw. You can also find yourself overstimulated and overwhelmed by all the content you are absorbing without having the chance to analyze or even really enjoy it. Sometimes, you may unwittingly expose yourself to traumatic or negative content that makes you anxious or depressed.

When you are constantly on social media and seeing how other people present their lives as glamorous and perfect, it's easy to feel pressured to live your life in a certain way or to try and convince others that your life is equally glamorous and perfect, even if what you are pretending to live is inauthentic and untrue to who you are. It's easy to forget that the content you see on social media is often curated and does not reflect reality, and yet there you are, putting yourself under pressure to live up to an illusion and letting that illusion make you feel inadequate. This will obviously take a knock at your confidence and may leave you feeling anxious or depressed.

The constant need for validation from online viewers and the pressure to be seen living a particular lifestyle can make you feel isolated and left out. You may see people living it up and in a way that you aren't able to or find that people aren't validating you the way you would've liked in your posts, and you may start questioning your self-worth because of this.

For some people, their use of social media becomes excessive and obsessive not because they post and engage with others on these platforms, but because they develop this fear of missing out on the latest trends, news, and other updates on these sites. The constant need to pick up a device and keep up with updates that happen in the millions per second is not only exhausting and impossible, it can also cause or exacerbate anxiety. When your focus is on the happenings of the Internet, you will be distracted from performing well at work or at school, and this can have negative effects on not only your current performance but your future as well.

Another prominent side effect of social media has become cyber bullying, especially with teenagers and young adults. People on the Internet can be ruthless with their criticism and harassment of others because the Internet provides a shield of anonymity. It has become common for people to find themselves the center of targeted and ongoing harassment and bullying, which can lead to anxiety and depressive episodes. These people may find themselves engaging in dangerous behaviors either as a way to cope with the bullying or to appease and hopefully stop the harassment.

With all these detrimental outcomes that come with social media use, it's important to learn how to reset the way you interact with these platforms and set boundaries for yourself around how you use and engage with content on them. Social media can consume your life, and so it's important to pull back and take some time offline to reestablish and strengthen your real-world connections, to find out what it is that you like and think without the influence and gaze of millions of people who are waiting to pounce on the first ideological or social faux pas you make. You can use that time to think about what you would like to use social media for—something that will enrich your life and your experiences online. Think about the kind of content you have been consuming online and how it has affected your mental health and your relationship with yourself. When you take a week offline, you'll realize just how much time you've been wasting online, and you will find yourself making time to take part in your hobbies, spend time with family, go to therapy if necessary, and generally do things that have a positive impact on you.

For some people, going completely cold turkey for a week from social media is too drastic because of how accustomed they've become to having it as a part of their lives. If you are one of these people, then finding ways to gradually limit your time online is the best way to reset your social media use. You can do this by turning your phone off during certain times when you find yourself distracted by social media. Maybe your phone will be off for a certain amount of hours while you are at school or work or when you are spending time with family and friends. Or you can switch off your social media notifications to limit your compulsion to look online the moment you hear that tone or see those red notifications screaming for your attention. Another helpful method is to track exactly how many hours you spend on social media. Sometimes being faced with the cold, hard figures of your social media screen time can be a sobering realization that motivates you to find more productive ways to spend your time. A lot of phones have this feature pre-programmed, or you can download an app that keeps track of these numbers for you.

Maximizing Internet Use

While the Internet can hinder our mental health and have a negative effect on our relationships with ourselves and others, it also carries a wealth of knowledge and resources that we can use to enrich our lives in many ways.

You can take part in online courses to improve your skills in your areas of interest. Some courses even offer certification for the knowledge you've gained that you can put on your resume. You can also find websites that can help with your schoolwork through extra classes and activities. Or you could want to learn how to play a new sport or some new hobby that you want to try out. There is nothing you cannot find on the Internet—all you have to do is look.

Some creative people find their inspiration in the work of others online. This can be for something small and personal like finding creative and unique gift ideas for loved ones, doing a DIY project at home, or other artistic endeavors. You can look on social media platforms for tips and tricks on how to execute your ideas and may even find new and improved ways to do things or find inspiration to improve what you had already planned to do.

If you find yourself struggling with a certain aspect of your life, you can find websites, videos, and other resources dedicated to helping people with the same issues. You can also find support groups and build an online community of support with people that understand what you're going through and can offer you practical tips and an ear to listen. This can be particularly helpful if you feel isolated and alone in your problem.

If you are someone with a business or a niche interest that you would love to explore, then the Internet is a great way for you to network with people that are actively involved in the work or interest you would like to expand your knowledge or skills in. You can use social media to easily market your business to people across the globe.

If you are a charitable person, then you use the Internet to raise funds for causes that are close to your heart and connect with organizations that are working for those causes and maybe even get involved in the work they are already doing.

If you are an activist and you want to help fight injustice and raise awareness about the struggles of others, then social media can be a powerful tool for you to amplify your voice and that of those whose fights for justice and truth you feel need to be heard across the world. We have seen in recent years the power that online protesting has in connecting the world against wrongs done against a person or a group of people and acting as a catalyst for change in the real world.

Of course, there will always be dangers to using the Internet, particularly for young people and teenagers who may be exposed to harmful or inappropriate content. That is where placing restrictions and boundaries on your usage comes in handy.

While the Internet has the potential to get in the way of our mental health and overall well-being, it can be a valuable resource when we use it to gather information that would allow us to improve our current skills and widen our knowledge about things that might help us cope.

The amazing, yet sometimes daunting, thing about life is that it consists of every single moment of our existence: every coffee date and commute to your daily destination, every conversation with loved ones, every evening spent in front of the TV, and every second you spend not enjoying what's right in front of you because you're already worried about the future. Before you know it, years will have gone by without you having any memory of them because your mind was either in a dark and anxious place, or you were so focused on tomorrow that you forgot to soak it in the little moments and make memories.

When you allow yourself to learn new ways to exist within your own mind so that you can show up differently in the world, you give yourself the chance to live a full and healthy life, and you allow the people around you to experience you as you were truly meant to be experienced: as a whole and complex being.

Chapter 4:

Dealing With Worry and Anxiety in

Specific Areas

Teenagers and young adults find themselves in an interesting place in life where it seems that everything they've known and understood about the world begins to fall away and they are suddenly faced with an alien world. The way that people interact with them changes. They find themselves having to make decisions for their futures that may have long-lasting effects on their lives. They discover new ideas and ways of living that entice and excite them. All these changes are met with the sobering reality of a rapidly changing world, one that challenges the most basic notions that mankind has held as sacrosanct truths for decades, even millennia.

It may be impossible to tackle every single thing that causes anxiety and stress in teenagers and young adults, but we can look at some of the most common areas where you will be exposed to worry and anxiety throughout your life. Our needs as humans do not change; we all want to have healthy relationships with our loved ones and to set positive goals for ourselves and actually achieve them. It is normal to worry about our futures and to have a desire to be as prepared for the changes of life as possible. That desire for certainty is what makes us human.

Academic Concerns

A common area of concern for people is whether they will have good grades and the anxiety that comes with doing well in all the tests, exams, projects, and so on that make up that final grade. We can define academic anxiety as the feeling you get when you are stressed out and fearful as a result of the pressures you have from school.

You could experience academic anxiety when you have to stand in front of your class or the entire school in order to give a speech, performance, or presentation. Or maybe you're anxious because it's test week and you're worried about whether you have had enough time to prepare well for all your assessments. For some people, any interactions that involve a subject that isn't exactly their strong suite can cause feelings of anxiety. So, whether you have to go to that subject's class or complete an assignment for it, you may find that you start experiencing those sensations your body produces when your stress levels are on the rise.

Having to perform within a specific time also adds on to a person's anxiety, particularly when there's a lot riding on your performance, like in a final examination of Scholastic Assessment Tests (SATs). It can sometimes feel like the bar for academic performance is too high, and you may go through periods when you doubt your intelligence and your ability to meet the demands of your schoolwork.

All of these different academic scenarios can trigger different levels of anxiety for each person depending on individual triggers. Mild levels of anxiety are healthy and can actually give you a better chance at doing well in your academics because you are focused. Being worried about your academics can get you to stop procrastinating and actually studying or preparing for an assignment properly. That level of stress and worry is usually temporary and goes away once you've started preparing for the task in question or while you are doing the task. However, you can also experience the kind of academic anxiety that makes it impossible for you to perform because you are mentally overwhelmed, or your body's response to the anxiety is so intense that you can't power through it.

Active Learning

You can combat your academic anxiety by making sure that you attend your classes and that you are focused and involved during the lessons and the activities you are given to apply what you've learned. Most teachers and instructors make use of active learning during lessons, which means that they provide you with case studies, encourage you to take part in discussions about the topic at hand, and even have you create things by applying your newly acquired knowledge. It might suck having to do small homework assignments or projects that aren't even for marks, but it's a great way to get you engaged with the material so that it comes to life. If you take part in active learning, you are more likely to retain what you are being taught, which in turn makes you less anxious when the time comes for your performance to be assessed and graded.

Get Curious and Explore Your Academics Outside of the Set Framework

Getting curious about the material can reduce your academic anxiety in the long run as well. Take some initiative and explore beyond what you are taught in the classroom. Now, how you do that is different for each person and will depend on what your interests are. If you are an avid reader, then you can do some research on the application of whatever you've been taught. Maybe you can even find different explanations and examples in your readings—examples that make it easier for you to understand the concepts you were taught. If you're into visual learning and application, then maybe do some science experiments or some re-enactments of historical moments. This is an extension of active learning in that it requires active participation and some enthusiasm on your part.

Taking Extra Lessons

Finally, you can run miles ahead of your anxiety if you just go the extra mile in order to understand your work so that you're more comfortable with it. Watch educational videos on the Internet, do extra activities and ask your instructor to help you through them, or form a study group with the A student in the course. The saying "Practice makes perfect" is popular for a reason. It works. The more you try at something, the better you become.

Social Concerns

Everyone has doubts and concerns about how they engage with people and their social standing in general. Prolonged and increasing concerns about this can turn into a disorder known as social anxiety disorder (SAD). Research studies done by the National Collaborating Centre for Mental Health (2013) have shown that SAD, or social phobia, is one the most common mental health issues in the world. Unfortunately, a lot of people don't look for professional help with their social phobia, and that's because our society tends to shame people that struggle with being social. If you are a shy or reserved person, people often talk about you with a condescending pity and always bring it up as a way to negatively affect how other people see you. In a world where being extroverted and overly confident is desired and socially rewarded, it can be difficult to exist as an introverted, shy, or reserved person.

Don't Do Things That Take You Out of Your Character

When you suffer from social anxiety, it's very common to find yourself taking part in activities that you don't enjoy because you want to fit in. When you are overly conscious of how people perceive you, and you believe that you will be judged negatively if you are yourself, then your primary concern in any social space is to fit in or, at the very least, to not stand out. So, when the group consensus is that everyone enjoys bungee jumping, for example, you'll probably go along with it even though you are deathly afraid of heights. I want to highlight that it's not a bad thing to get out of your comfort zone and try new things, but stepping out of your character in order to fit in does more harm than good. You will be representing yourself as someone you are not and you will have to deal with the stress of maintaining that lie and the constant fear of being caught out. It's probably not a good idea to deal with your social anxiety by adding more stress to your life.

Avoid Negative Coping Mechanisms

It's a common approach for people that are overwhelmed to try and numb themselves from their social anxiety. They can find themselves drowning their fears in alcohol, drug use, and other forms of substance abuse.

Use Cognitive Reframing

Questioning your thoughts and beliefs and examining them against the lens of logic and hard evidence is a great way to tackle your social anxiety. More often than not, what you fear the most is unlikely to happen, and even if it did, it would not be as world shattering as you've built it up to be in your mind.

Face Your Social Fears Head-on

Facing your social anxiety and learning how to manage it is probably the best way to get started. It's nearly impossible to avoid people all together, and living with the fear of interacting with people makes your world so much smaller and dimmer than it needs ro be. When you learn how to manage your social anxiety, you open yourself up to a world of new opportunities, experiences, and people that will enrich your life and value you as you are.

Challenge yourself to take small steps to tackle your social anxiety every now and then. It can be something like answering a question in class or at work, making small talk with your doorman or the janitor that you run into every day, or hosting a small dinner party with your friends and asking them to invite a friend or two that you don't know. Slowly teaching yourself to socialize with people you don't know helps you improve your socialization skills and gives you the confidence to go and put yourself out there more often.

Shift Your Focus From Yourself to the Other Person

Experts suggest that one of the most effective ways to deal with social anxiety is to shift your focus away from yourself and onto the people around you. People suffering from social anxiety are hyper-aware of all their perceived faults and flaws, constantly assessing and remarking on every word they say and every reaction they receive from others and replaying what they could have done differently. It's no wonder, then, that interacting with people can be physically and mentally exhausting for them. The thing about having all your focus squarely lasered on yourself is that you completely miss the people and interactions around you. When you're listening to people simply to react, and not to hear and process what they're saying, you can miss a lot of nuance and opportunities to authentically connect with others. In fact, you're more likely to cast yourself as the social outcast when you're hyper focused on yourself because you come off as aloof and disinterested in creating real relationships.

In contrast, when you shift your focus to the other person, you give them the sense that you're really interested in connecting with them and that person is more likely to enjoy speaking with you and may even overlook the minor faux pas you make during the conversation because they feel seen and valued. People love talking about themselves, and they love it even more when you show that you are engaged in what they're saying. When you do this, you come across as more relatable because you're present in the conversation instead of worrying about your perceived flaws.

Rename Your Interactions With Your Social Anxiety

Having social anxiety usually starts with people using your quiet or reserved nature to label you. The negative connotations that people attach to these attributes makes you feel like they are negative traits to have, and that is how social anxiety develops. If you are constantly told that you are this bad thing that is negative, you begin to internalize that, and soon you don't want to be in social settings because you've been made to believe that your attributes are negative and undesirable.

The one thing you can do is to detach your feelings from your identity. Your feelings and thoughts are temporary, and although they may influence how you perceive things or how you act, they don't define you as a person. So, instead of letting yourself be nervous about going to an office party, you can focus on the fact that you will get to interact with your favorite colleague outside of the office and pump yourself up for seeing your colleagues outside of the workspace, where they will be free to be themselves.

Financial Concerns

We are currently living in highly unfavorable and volatile economic times. Salaries are stagnant, the cost of living is constantly increasing, and there are talks of a looming inflation. It's no wonder that a lot of people are under a lot of stress about their finances. This stress is far higher for people that have lower incomes because they are more exposed to the negative effects of an unstable economy. Moreover, they have to do a lot more planning and restructuring if they want to free up money to afford things and meet their needs. Unfortunately, being in a tight financial situation also means that you are less likely to afford the things that can help you cope with your financial stress, such as therapy, or even investing in a project that can generate more income for you.

Research done by Reinecke in 2022 found that almost 70% of teenagers said that their post-graduation plans were affected by their concerns on financing their higher education amidst the rising costs of going to college. If you are a part of these teens, then you are probably concerned about the prospect of getting a student loan to pay for your higher education and how you'll be able to pay it off. Social discourse is filled with people being open and transparent about their struggles to pay off their student debt and how this affects their lives and their finances. You may also be concerned about choosing the right career because you don't want to find yourself investing years in a career path that won't translate into financial success.

For young adults, you're transitioning into a space where your financial responsibilities are increasing, and you may find yourself completely financially self-reliant for the first time. A lot of the blinders you had about finances come off suddenly and dramatically. I, for one, was shocked at the reality of what it takes to finance your own life when I stepped into young adulthood. There were a lot of things that I had taken for granted because they were always around. And I was astounded at the price of almost everything! This was especially true when I had to furnish my very first apartment. The price of rugs, beds, and such blew me away. I soon found myself keeping a close eye on how long I left the heat on and whether I had left any unnecessary lights on. All of these behaviors that I had found annoying from my parents were suddenly brought into sharp perspective.

Take a Realistic Look at Your Financial Status

If you have serious concerns about your finances, the best thing you can do for yourself is to take a realistic look at your finances and see where you currently are, where you would need to be, and how you can change certain behaviors to improve your spending. Auditing your finances every now and then can help you identify money pits in your life. Budgeting is an important skill that can help you maximize your money and teach you healthy spending habits. The sooner you teach yourself how to budget effectively, the better your money management will be.

When you have an effective budget in place, you're easily able to cut out any wasteful expenditure and identify the things that you need to prioritize. These will depend on your financial goals.

Look Into Creating an Extra Source of Income

There has been a lot of talk about extra sources of income in recent years. This is mainly because most people can no longer afford to live a comfortable lifestyle on their monthly salaries alone. If you want to allay some of your financial concerns, then perhaps it's time you also do some research and find ways that you can monetize your skills.

While the Internet is saturated with articles and videos about selling digital products, affiliate marketing, and other such things, I advise that you focus on finding things that align with your interests and skills. Adding a source of income means setting aside more time to work on that source, and that can be difficult if you already have a full plate. Doing something that you have some sort of love or passion for will make those long nights easier to go through. Lastly, you want to create something that can evolve and grow with you, something that's sustainable.

Career Concerns

Career concerns are closely intertwined with financial concerns because for a lot of people, the trajectory of their career has huge financial implications for their lives. The better you perform at work, the more likely you are to be rewarded with a promotion and a better salary. Likewise, the more skilled you are and the more money you invest into developing your skills, the higher your chances are of advancing your career and hitting those career milestones that you've set out for yourself.

Our careers are an especially unique area of concern because it's so difficult to separate your performance from your identity. Generally, your value at work is determined by how well you perform, and this has only gotten worse with the rise of influencer culture and the prevalence of placing yourself as a brand and not just another worker in a company. It's, therefore, understandable that a lot of people view performance reviews as a measure of their personal worth.

For those who are still trying to find the right career for themselves, there can be concern about finding something that you're passionate about and provides stability and financial success. We've seen an increase in the rise of unconventional and new career options that seem to be far more financially fruitful than conventional careers. A lot of influencers, YouTubers, streamers, and gamers are outearning lawyers, accounts, and teachers by a large stretch. And while the success of these careers can be enticing, there are people who are concerned about the longevity of these relatively new jobs that are reliant on platforms that may come and go.

On the other hand, you can find yourself worried about investing time and money preparing to join a conventional career path only for it to fizzle out before you've had a chance to cement yourself and create a stable financial base for yourself.

Wherever you find yourself, here are some strategies you can implement in your life when you feel your career anxiety rising.

Take Stock of Your Strengths and Skills

When you're constantly on the move in your work days, and the only time you get to take note of your achievements and your growth is during a performance review, it can be difficult to be aware of your strengths and skills and to give yourself a pat on the back for all the hours and passion you've put into your work. A good practice I recommend is to keep a document open on your PC where you reflect on your achievements. You'll be surprised at how far your skills have taken you, and constantly reflecting on that can help you keep your confidence high.

Look to the Future

Finally, look at your career in the long-term so that you don't make drastic decisions based on temporary circumstances and emotions. If you're worried about a performance review, remind yourself that it's one of hundreds of reviews that you will go to. If you get a negative review, it's not the end of the world; you can try again next month or next quarter. Also, remind yourself that you've gone through this before—you made it through then, and you'll do it again.

If you're worried about choosing the right career for yourself, remember that you have a lifetime to land in the right space. If you focus on harnessing your passions and honing your skills in alignment with those passions, you'll be fine whether you choose to go the conventional route or down the road less taken. You can transfer your skills to different roles in different industries. Remember that these skills can take you wherever you need them and the only limitation there is your mind and your ambition.

Global Concerns

The world seems to be in a strangely transitional phase where our environment is falling apart, major wars are being waged across the globe, and everything just generally feels like it's headed toward doom. In short, it seems like it's not a great time to be a young person. Two of the most pressing global concerns that young people have are climate change and war.

Climate Change

Research has shown that a lot of young people are anxious about climate change and feel that their governments are failing them (Pruitt-Young, 2021). A lot of governments are not making substantial and long-term policy commitments towards tackling climate change. For those few that make such policy commitments, there's almost never any actual follow-up. It almost seems as if these policies and public proclamations are merely performances by governments to silence their citizens.

Over the past few years, there has been a sharp criticism of world leaders that flock to international conferences in private jets to proclaim their concerns about the environment and assure us that they're doing everything in their power to combat climate change. Yet, their actions undercut those noble sentiments. The Pruitt- Young study found a direct correlation between young people's beliefs that their governments are not doing enough to deal with the climate crisis and their feelings of worry and stress.

If you're part of these young people, there are a few things you can do to ease your climate anxiety.

Raise Awareness

Social media has proven itself to be a powerful tool that can be used to amplify important issues and bring them to the attention of millions of people across the globe. So, consider using your platform as a means to raise awareness about the issues surrounding climate change and how everyone can contribute their time and efforts toward preserving and protecting the environment. You don't have to start big and want to win over millions to the cause. You can start with little projects and campaigns and such that are specifically targeted toward your immediate community. Starting with a smaller area of focus and letting that engagement naturally spread is a great way to build momentum and ensure that you develop your skills in raising awareness.

Get Involved

There are already a number of organizations and initiatives around the world that are committed to tackling climate change and have done real work toward that goal. Take charge of your concerns by getting involved in one of them. You can help these organizations raise funds for their various projects, or you can contribute your time and volunteer to help out with the work they're doing in and around communities. Maybe you'll find that a specific organization whose work you admire has not established a solid base in your part of the world yet, and you could be part of the team that helps to expand their work to the communities around you.

Make Changes to Your Lifestyle

One of the biggest challenges in the fight against climate change is human consumption. We're living in times where consumerism and hyper-consumption are at an all-time high. You can make a difference by making changes to reduce waste and overconsumption. For example, look into using public transport instead of a private car everyday as a way to reduce carbon emissions in the atmosphere. Make sustainable food and fashion choices by reducing your spending on products that use an unreasonable amount of packaging and clothing that isn't durable. You can also implement recycling in your household's waste system to ensure that everything that can be repurposed is not wasted and the things that have to be thrown away are handled responsibly.

War

Another common cause of global concern for young people is war anxiety. We see horrific images of wars and the destruction they're causing to families, cities, economies, and so on. Every day there's new information about the deaths of innocent civilians, and having to see the trauma of others makes you acutely aware of how easily you could find your country embroiled in the same situation. Being anxious when you see images of war-torn countries is a reasonable and all too common response. The American Psychological Association conducted a poll in 2022 where 80% of the participants reported being significantly stressed as a result of the Russian-Ukraine war.

Wars have a particularly concentrated effect on the world's economy, and that effect is felt by every country in the world. Our current systems run on financing, and you can't do much in this world that doesn't involve money. Being preoccupied about the wars is sensible because it means you understand the enormous impact that these wars have on our lives.

It can feel like there is no way to escape war anxiety because there isn't much you can do to stop the wars, but there are a few ways that you can break out of your anxiety.

Cultivate Kindness and Compassion

War anxiety often makes people angry. The anger is often caused by the observation of injustices being done to innocent civilians in the name of a war they don't even support, or it can be directed at the people and institutions that are in support of and funding a war. Anger is an extremely volatile emotion that demands to be felt at a moment's notice. Unfortunately, it's very common for people to express their anger on the wrong people, and this is especially true in this case. So, instead of letting your anger build up and spill over on the wrong people, you can instead focus your energy on cultivating kindness and compassion. You can do this by talking to people with different perspectives on the issue and trying to understand these views and drawing on the positive aspects thereof. You can also choose to focus on the joy and kindness that you see around you, and be intentional about being part of that joy and paying it forward.

Limit Your Media Exposure

Absorbing news about the wars currently waged in the world can become addictive because you'll find yourself wanting to constantly be updated on all the latest developments, watching documentaries to gain a fuller view of what's happening on the ground and so on. Try to limit how much media you expose yourself to each day so that you can break the cycle of your war anxiety. Putting a set time for yourself to read through the news each day is a great place to start. Also, try not to reach for your phone or news channel first thing in the morning or right before you go to bed. Instead, try setting a good tone for your day and ending on an equally positive note by having a morning and night routine that brings you joy.

Create an Interactive Routine

Limiting your exposure to the media means that you'll suddenly find yourself with a considerable amount of free time. It's easy for your mind to wander back to whatever troubling news you last read or saw during this time; you'll find your anxiety peaking again, and you'll be tempted to go back online for more updates. Once you've chosen to limit your exposure, it'll help you to create a new routine for yourself that keeps your mind busy with things that are productive and positive. Maybe you could start going to the gym, spending time getting that passion project of yours off the ground, or starting a new hobby.

Anxiety makes itself known in every aspect of our lives and it can sometimes feel like there is no escape. But with what you've picked up so far, you should realize that there are actually a number of ways to deal with your anxiety, and that it doesn't have to consume your life.

No matter which area of life makes you feel anxious, you can break that cycle simply by being proactive and intentional with your response to it. There's always a way out of unhealthy levels of anxiety, but the first step is always the hardest because you have to face the cause of your anxiety and be honest with yourself about why you're anxious. Once you've moved past that hurdle, you'll find it easier to think of ways to redirect your energy and focus elsewhere.

Chapter 5:

Exercises

A person cannot be anxious and relaxed at the same time. Trying to fight your anxiety instead of understanding it will only make the battle twice as hard. Instead of trying to stop yourself from being anxious, I'm going to give you some final tips and tricks that you can use to help you lean into and learn from your anxiety.

We've discussed at length how anxiety affects both the mind and body. Because you find yourself mentally and physically dysregulated when you're anxious, the most effective exercises to try are those that pull your mind and body out of that state of dysregulation by firmly planting you in the present. Your mind can wander into any number of directions at any given time, but your body is only ever here in the present. So, it follows that if you want to reconnect your body to the now, your best bet is to follow exercises that bring about an awareness of your physical state and all its sensation, while roping the mind back into the present with you.

Emotion Regulation Techniques

When you are in a state of emotional dysregulation, you'll find it difficult to process your emotions and even harder to control your behavior because the dysregulation takes over.

When you think about something or experience something that causes you stress, your mind responds to that thing by latching onto and even creating a lot of negative thoughts around it. This increases your stress levels and sends your body into stress-response mode. Now your mind and body are both dysregulated, and the automatic response here for most people is to latch onto behaviors that help us avoid the root cause of the stress or engage with it in unhealthy and unproductive ways. When you struggle to control your emotions, your reaction to most stressors is often too big and too destructive when looked at through the lens of the root cause. So, your response often makes the situation ten times worse than what it should have been. In order to avoid that, it's important that you learn how to regulate your emotions before you find yourself engaged in destructive and unproductive behaviors.

Learning how to regulate your emotions in the moment is hard, more so for people whose emotional dysregulation has developed into diagnosable mental health disorders, such as bipolar disorder, post-traumatic stress disorder (PTSD), attention deficit hyperactivity disorder (ADHD), and others. People who suffer from these and other associated disorders usually have a higher emotional sensitivity than most and are prone to unstable moods or emotions. Because they were not equipped with the proper emotional regulation strategies to help them deal with their emotional sensitivity in a constructive way, their maladaptive responses to stress and anxiety led to disordered behaviors over time.

Breathing Exercises

Breathing exercises are a great way to anchor yourself to the present because you can only ever breathe in the now. Here are a few step-by-step breakdowns of different breathing exercises that you can try when you're feeling emotionally dysregulated.

5-4-3-2-1 Method

The 5-4-3-2-1 method is one that slowly pulls you into the present. Its brilliance lies in this: It slowly engages all of your senses. The first step is to become aware and mindful of your breathing. Take a few slow and deliberate breaths to bring your body out of its automatic regulation of your breathing. Once you've settled into this awareness of your breath, engage your mind and bring it into awareness with your environment by doing the following:

1. Engage your sense of sight by identifying five different things that you can see. You can do this by noticing five different colors around you or five objects that are not related to each other. I personally love textures, so when I practice this method, I will try and identify five different textures in my environment. I like to linger on each texture by trying to define it as I see it.

2. Engage your sense of touch by identifying four things that you can touch around you. For most people, this is when they will identify different textures in a room. What I like to do during this step is to move around my environment and literally touch every textured piece that I have identified and describe what it feels like under my fingers to myself. This is a great way to also release some of that muscle tension that's built up during your fight-or-flight response.

3. Engage your hearing by listening for three different things that you can hear. Don't engage in what you hear; just observe it as a sound in your environment.

4. Engage your sense of smell by noticing two things that you can smell around you. Perhaps there's coffee brewing nearby or a delicious meal being prepared. Or how about the scent wafting off of your skin or your hair?

5. Engage your taste buds by noticing one thing that you can taste. This one can be a bit tricky if you haven't really had anything to eat or drink recently. Maybe you have a piece of candy in your pocket or on your desk that you can pop into your mouth.

With each of these steps, remember to continuously take slow, deliberate breaths so that your mind doesn't wander off on a tangent again. You may be tempted to rush through these steps or to let your mind off on a tangent when one of your engaged senses has triggered a happy memory that you would like to explore further. Remember that these steps are not merely boxes to be ticked so that you can rush off to the next task. The purpose is to calm your mind and bring your body out of its fight-or-flight mode. So, take your time with each step;

let your senses fully awaken at each step. If you need to redo the steps again because you still feel a bit wired and out of touch with your body, do so.

Box Breathing

Box breathing is a simple, quick, and highly effective breathing exercise that can help bring your body out of fight-or-flight mode and restore a sense of calm to your mind. The method has four basic steps:

1. Breathe in

2. Hold your breath

3. Breathe out

4. Hold your breath

The exercise gets its name from the box-shaped manner in which you will control your breathing. Each step is meant to last for equal counts of three to four seconds each, resembling a box. You can hold each step for longer counts if you wish, or repeat the exercise a few times until you feel your body releasing some of that tension. The idea behind box breathing is to bring your natural breathing style to your focus in moments of stress. This is a great technique to use if one of your anxiety markers is shortness of breath.

It's recommended that this technique is most effective if you do it sitting comfortably in an upright position with your eyes closed. Try to focus on the feeling of your stomach muscles expanding and contracting as you breathe in and out, but don't engage the muscles. Just let them rhythmically move in and out and notice how that slight movement makes your mind and body feel. You will notice that the longer you do this, the more you can feel a release of tension from your shoulders.

Belly Breathing

Belly breathing, or diaphragmatic breathing, is a breathing technique that is most useful to people who find that their heart rate and blood pressure dramatically increase when they are under immense stress or having an anxiety attack. The diaphragm is a large muscle that is situated right between the base of your lungs and the top of your belly. This muscle helps regulate how much oxygen your lungs inhale and exhale. This technique is more engaging because it needs you to lie flat on your back, preferably with your head supported and your knees bent. You can also do it sitting on a flat surface with your knees bent, but it's most effective when you're lying down.

Once you've found a comfortable starting position, relax your shoulders by rolling them upwards, to the back, and then downwards. Next, put one hand on your belly and another on your chest. These are the two areas where you will feel your body expand and contract as the air moves through you. Putting your hands on them helps you focus on that movement of the body. Then, gently breathe in through your nose, taking in as much oxygen as you can so that your lungs are fully expanded. Really feel the air as it fills your body. Next, you'll purse your lips as if whistling or drinking from a straw and slowly exhale until you can feel your stomach completely contracted.

Repeat these steps until you can feel your heart rate slowly returning to its natural rhythm. This technique doesn't place any limit on how long you are meant to inhale or exhale because the focus is on the belly and the diaphragm. Each person's lung capacity differs, so where it takes you thirteen seconds to fill your lungs to their capacity, it may take someone else only five seconds.

Resonant Breathing

Resonant breathing is a breathing exercise that aims to bring your nervous, respiratory, and cardio-vascular systems back in sync so that they can function at optimal capacity. Because we have control over our breathing frequency, we can bring our other systems to the same frequency through controlled breathing.

To get started, lie or sit down in a comfortable position, preferably one where your torso is not slouched or overly extended. Then take a gentle breath through the nose for about six seconds, and make sure that your mouth is closed. Make sure not to fill your lungs with air all the way. Then, slowly exhale through the mouth for about six seconds as well. Your inhalation and exhalation counts can be longer or shorter depending on your comfort level. Remember that the goal is to breathe in and out as gently as you can so that you can create a nice and slow frequency for your other systems to fall into. It usually takes about 10 to 12 minutes for your other bodily systems to break out of their flight-or-flight response mode and join the frequency of your breath. You can listen to some calming music or focus on the sounds around you while you wait for your body to regulate.

Movement Exercises

Moving your body and getting all the tension that builds up during the fight-or-flight response to flow and eventually be released from the body is a great way to regulate your emotional response. When you're physically active and releasing tension, your body gets the message that you're dealing with whatever threat triggered your stress response, so it stops releasing the stress hormones, and it becomes easier for you to return to a regulated and calm state. The physical movement doesn't have to be intense; it just needs to be enough that the tension leaves your body. The best way to do this is by targeted exercises in the areas that are carrying your tension at that moment.

Neck and Shoulder Rolls

People commonly carry tension in their necks and their spines when they're under stress. Neck rolls are a great way to release that tension without having to do too much physical movement.

To start, sit upright and make sure that your spine is comfortably extended and supported. Start by rolling your neck in a full circle. You may gradually extend your neck to release as much tension as you can, but don't strain yourself, and only extend it as far as you're comfortable. Next, arch your shoulders forward, gently roll them up and backwards, and then push them back down again. You can do these two exercises together or in isolation, whatever works best for you. The important thing is to slowly feel the tension flowing and being released. Be careful not to overstretch or to move too fast because that could hurt you. As you do these neck and shoulder rolls, you'll start hearing some snaps and cracks as the tension knots begin loosening up.

Muscle Tension and Release

Sometimes your body stores tension in your jaw, wrists, legs, and so on. The best way to release this tension is by engaging these muscle groups through tension and release exercises. During these exercises, you inhale as you slightly tense up the targeted muscle group until you can feel a slight pull that confirms that the muscles are engaged. Hold that for a few seconds, and then exhale as you disengage the muscle and allow for a tension release. You can do this for a few minutes, giving yourself about 30 seconds between each exercise so that the muscles can rest.

If the tension is in your jaw and cheeks, open your mouth as wide as can and make sure that the jaw is unlocked. If your chest is carrying the tension, try arching back and forth with pauses in between each action. Wherever your tension lies, move your body around that particular muscle group so that you're aware of how to engage the muscle. Then proceed to do repetitions of tension and release in those areas until you can feel a reduction in tension there.

Rhythmic Movement

Our bodies have a natural internal rhythm that keeps all of our bodily functions in sync, and when our emotions are dysregulated, this internal rhythm is brought into chaos. Engaging in rhythmic movement can help bring the body and the mind back in sync with one another.

There are a number of things you can do that are a rhythmic movement. The first thing that comes to mind is dancing. Putting on a good song and dancing your troubles away can help release physical tension and draw your mind out of its overwhelmed state, thus promoting emotional regulation. You can also try playing an instrument or rhythmically tapping your hands and stomping your feet. Or you can take a walk around your neighborhood and intentionally match the pace of your steps to that of your breaths. Any form of physical movement can be rhythmic if you want it to be, and it's a great way to get both the mind and body involved in a common purpose that brings them in touch with one another.

Conclusion

Don't underestimate the power of vision and direction. These are irresistible forces, able to transform what might appear to be unconquerable obstacles into traversable pathways and expanding opportunities. –Jordan B. Peterson

Making changes in your life is not an easy thing to do. You have to resist your body's fear of the unknown and commit to being resilient against the thoughts and behaviors that may have once served you well but are now standing in the way of you living a rich and fulfilling life. You've taken the first steps toward making those changes, and I hope that you will stay committed to the cause and never lose that spark that motivates you to keep striving for better.

Now that we're at the end of our journey, I hope that you've started trying out the different techniques and methods that have been shown to combat your anxiety. Start small so that you don't get overwhelmed or discouraged.

This journey will be long, so don't feel bad if you find yourself struggling to get past certain hurdles. Remember that you are undoing years of learned behavior, automatic responses, and thought patterns. You're essentially working toward rewriting the neural pathways that have formed in your brain over all these years, and that's quite a task. In those moments of struggle, be kind and gentle with yourself and know that one bad day doesn't outdo months or even years of progress. After all, each step forward is a step further from the past.

The most important takeaway you should have is this: Fear is something that never completely goes away. It's a key part of our genetic makeup that helps keep us alive and prepared when danger presents itself. And so, your goal should never be to eradicate fear; it should be about learning how to control your fear and use it to your advantage. In that spirit, remember to give yourself the space and grace to feel your emotions without judgment or fear. Hold a candle toward them and look at them with understanding as they pour out of you.

Everything you've been taught in this book starts with being present and allowing yourself to feel what is going on within and around you. That's not by accident. Fear feeds anxiety, and if you're afraid to look within and stare directly at what scares you, then you'll never win the battle against your anxiety. Likewise, if you're going to fight and run from whatever you find looking back at you, you won't win. Remember that whatever you have hidden within yourself is a part of you. No matter how foreign it may look or feel, it's one with you and it won't destroy you. So, observe it with care and give it a soft landing spot to release its anger and hurt, knowing that you have to be there to care for it and respect it as a part of what makes you complex and whole.

The tools and skills you've learned in this book are not meant to be used as a Band-Aid to quickly cover up scary or uncomfortable emotions. They will only truly be effective if you apply them with intentionality and genuineness. And that means that sometimes you will find your feelings bubbling over despite your best efforts at regulating your emotions and calming your body. When this happens, think of it as a green flag and a testament to your growth. When we come across feelings that have been suppressed for a long time, they burst forth, packing a punch and demanding to be felt and seen.

No matter what happens on your journey to healing your anxiety, remember the vision that encouraged you to go this path, and keep it alive at the back of your mind. Working on yourself requires a daily recommitment to the cause, and for you to make it to the end, you have to get into it knowing that it'll exhaust and test you, but you're worth the effort.

Now is the time to take charge and make a real difference to the way you engage with your mind and body every single day. Remember that there's no shame in speaking your truth or seeking help and support from professionals, friends, and family. Having a community from which you can draw strength when you're in need of a little extra encouragement, validation, or even acknowledgement of your growth can make all the difference.

Congratulations on taking the reins of your mental health back, and good luck with your new and improved life!

Free Workbook

Help With Anxiety. Grab your freebie now: **https://BookHip.com/WQTTMXX**

References

Abraham, M. (2022, September 3). *Anxiety as the cause of muscle tension.* CalmClinic. www.calmclinic.com/anxiety/signs/muscle-tension

American Psychological Association. (2017, July). *What is cognitive behavioral therapy?* American Psychological Association. https://www.apa.org/ptsd-guideline/patients-and-families/cognitive-behavioral

Anxiety, depression, stress: Why the differences matter. (2017, September 28). Premier Health. www.premierhealth.com/your-health/articles/women-wisdom-wellness-/anxiety-depression-stress-why-the-differences-matter

Ascher, J. & Tonies, F. (2021, February 18). *How to turn everyday stress into 'optimal stress.'* McKinsey Quarterly. https://www.mckinsey.com/capabilities/people-and-organizational-performance/our-insights/how-to-turn-everyday-stress-into-optimal-stress

Barta, M. (2010, May). *What is academic anxiety?* Temecula Valley Unified School District. https://www.tvusd.k12.ca.us/cms/lib/CA02208611/Centricity/Domain/9537/4964104180009246281.pdf

Blanchfield, T. (2023, April 14). *What to know about internal family systems (IFS) therapy.* Verywell Mind. www.verywellmind.com/what-is-ifs-therapy-internal-family-systems-therapy-5195336

Caron, C. (2022, January 19). *The upside of anxiety.* The New York Times. www.nytimes.com/2022/01/19/well/mind/anxiety-benefits.html

Chapman, A.L. (2006, September 9). Dialectical behavior therapy: Current indications and unique elements. *Psychiatry (Edgmont),*

3(9), 62–68. www.ncbi.nlm.nih.gov/pmc/articles/PMC2963469/

Choice Theory / Reality Therapy. (2019, May 10). APA Center. www.apacenter.com/therapy-types/choice-theory-reality-therapy/

Cigna Staff. (2022, August). *Differentiating between worry, stress, and anxiety.* Cigna Singapore. www.cigna.com.sg/health-content-hub/mental-health/differentiating-between-stress-worry-anxiety

Cohut, M. (2019, August 30). *4 top tips for coping with social anxiety.* Medical News Today. www.medicalnewstoday.com/articles/326211

Contributors of WebMD Editorial. (2021, April 21). *What is gestalt therapy?* WebMD. www.webmd.com/mental-health/what-is-gestalt-therapy

Courtney, R. (n.d.). *Resonance frequency breathing.* Dr Rosalba Courtney. www.rosalbacourtney.com/resonance-frequency-breathing/

Dialectical behavioural therapy (DBT). (2020, December). Mind UK. www.mind.org.uk/information-support/drugs-and-treatments/talking-therapy-and-counselling/dialectical-behaviour-therapy-dbt/

Diaphragmatic breathing. (2022, March 30). Cleveland Clinic. my.clevelandclinic.org/health/articles/9445-diaphragmatic-breathing

Done right, Internet use among children can increase learning opportunities and build digital skills. (2019, November 27). UNICEF. www.unicef.org/press-releases/done-right-internet-use-among-children-can-increase-learning-opportunities-and-build

Duszynski-Goodman, L. (2023, April 28). *Mental health statistics.* Forbes Health. www.forbes.com/health/mind/mental-health-statistics/

Endorphins. (2022, May 19). Cleveland Clinic. my.clevelandclinic.org/health/body/23040-endorphins

Ferguson, S. (2022, September 12). *How to live in the moment and be more present.* PsychCentral. psychcentral.com/blog/what-it-really-means-to-be-in-the-present-moment

FPM Editors. (2021, February 15). *Using cognitive reframing to encourage behavior change.* American Academy of Family Physicians. www.aafp.org/pubs/fpm/blogs/inpractice/entry/cognitive_ref raming.html

The free energy principle explained. (n.d.). Restoring Balance. restoringbalance.life/2022/03/29/the-free-energy-principle-explained/

Friston, K. (2004). The free-energy principle: A rough guide to the brain? *Trends in Cognitive Sciences, 13*(7), 293–301.

Gillman, B. (2017, May 5). *The physical side of anxiety.* Intermountain Healthcare. intermountainhealthcare.org/blogs/topics/live-well/2017/05/the-physical-side-of-anxiety/

Goldman, R. (2020, July 1). *Understanding cognitive restructuring.* Verywell Mind. www.verywellmind.com/what-is-cognitive-restructuring-3024490

Gotter, A. (2023, March 22). *8 breathing exercises to try when you feel anxious.* Healthline. www.healthline.com/health/breathing-exercises-for-anxiety

Gottschalk, M.G., & Domschke, K. (2017). Genetics of generalized anxiety disorder and related traits. *Dialogues in Clinical Neuroscience, 19*(2), 159–168.

Henderson, R.K., et al. (2012). When does stress help or harm? The effects of stress controllability and subjective stress response on Stroop performance. *Frontiers in Psychology,* 3(3).

Horn, C.C. (2008). Why is the neurobiology of nausea and vomiting so important? *Appetite, 50*(2-3), 430–434.

Horton, H. (2023, January 13). *Private jet emissions quadrupled during Davos 2022.* The Guardian. www.theguardian.com/environment/2023/jan/13/private-jet-emissions-quadrupled-davos-2022

Jeurkar, R. (2018, May 7). *Anxious about your appraisal conversation? You can now prepare for it.* White Swan Foundation. www.whiteswanfoundation.org/workplace/anxious-about-your-appraisal-conversation-you-can-now-prepare-for-it

Jewell, T. & Hoshaw, C. (2022, December 2). What is *diaphragmatic breathing?* Healthline. www.healthline.com/health/diaphragmatic-breathing

Joseph, F. (2015, February 23). *Five ways you can use the Internet positively.* Passnownow. passnownow.com/5-ways-can-use-internet-positively/

Leonard, J. (2023, February 9). *What to know about anticipation anxiety.* Medical News Today. www.medicalnewstoday.com/articles/anticipatory-anxiety

Mayo Clinic Staff. (2017, September 27). *Depression and anxiety: Exercise eases symptoms.* Mayo Clinic. www.mayoclinic.org/diseases-conditions/depression/in-depth/depression-and-exercise/art-20046495

Mayo Clinic Staff. (2021, July 8). *Chronic stress puts your health at risk.* Mayo Clinic. www.mayoclinic.org/healthy-lifestyle/stress-management/in-depth/stress/art-20046037

Nichols, M.H. (2021). *Morgan Harper Nichols's Instagram photo: Whenever you start to feel overwhelmed.* Pinterest. www.pinterest.nz/pin/854628466797286565/

Nunez, K. (2021, June 17). *What is reality therapy and choice theory?* Healthline. www.healthline.com/health/reality-therapy

Overview - Cognitive behavioural therapy (CBT). (2022, November 10). NHS. www.nhs.uk/mental-health/talking-therapies-medicine-treatments/talking-therapies-and-counselling/cognitive-behavioural-therapy-cbt/overview/

Oxford Languages. (2023). *Dialectical - Google Search*. Google. www.google.com/search?q=dialectical&rlz=1C1GCEB_enZA 1047ZA1047&oq=diale&aqs=chrome.0.69i59l2j69i57j0i67i650j 0i67i131i433i650j69i60l3.2531j1j7&sourceid=chrome&ie=UTF -8

Panganiban, K. (2023, March 14). *Social media & relationships*. Choosing Therapy. www.choosingtherapy.com/social-media-relationships/

Perell, D. (n.d.). *Don't kill time. David Perell*. perell.com/essay/dont-kill-time/

Pikorn, I. (n.d.). *The 5-4-3-2-1 grounding technique: Manage anxiety by anchoring in the present*. Insight Timer. insighttimer.com/blog/54321-grounding-technique/

Psychology Today Staff. (n.d.). *What is anxiety?* Psychology Today. www.psychologytoday.com/za/basics/anxiety

Psychology Today Staff. (n.d.). *Gestalt therapy*. Psychology Today. www.psychologytoday.com/za/therapy-types/gestalt-therapy

Psychology Today Staff. (n.d.). *Internal family systems therapy*. Psychology Today. https://www.psychologytoday.com/za/therapy-types/internal-family-systems-therapy

Raypole, C. (2021, May 26). *Ready to overcome social anxiety? These 9 tips can help*. Healthline. www.healthline.com/health/anxiety/how-to-get-over-social-anxiety

Reinicke, C. (2022, June 1). *54% of teenagers feel unprepared to finance their futures, survey shows*. CNBC. www.cnbc.com/2022/06/01/54percent-of-teens-feel-unprepared-to-finance-their-futures-survey-shows.html

The Recovery Village. (2022, May 26). *Anxiety disorders facts and statistics.* The Recovery Village. www.therecoveryvillage.com/mental-health/anxiety/anxiety-disorder-statistics/

Robinson, L. & Smith, M. (2023, March 29). *Social media and mental health.* Help Guide. www.helpguide.org/articles/mental-health/social-media-and-mental-health.htm

Saner, E. (2022, December 15). *'I didn't realise how badly it affected me until I was off it': What it's like to have a social media detox.* The Guardian. www.theguardian.com/media/2022/dec/15/i-didnt-realise-how-badly-it-affected-me-until-i-was-off-it-should-more-of-us-try-a-social-media-detox

Santomauro, D. F., Herrera, A. M. M., Shadid, J., Zheng, P., Ashbaugh, C., Pigott, D. M., Abbafati, C., Adolph, C., Amlag, J. O., Aravkin, A. Y., Bang-Jensen, B. L., Bertolacci, G. J., Bloom, S. S., Castellano, R., Castro, E., Chakrabarti, S., Chattopadhyay, J., Cogen, R. M., Collins, J. K., & Dai, X. (2021). Global prevalence and burden of depressive and anxiety disorders in 204 countries and territories in 2020 due to the COVID-19 pandemic. *The Lancet, 398*(10312), 1700–1712.

Schimelpfening, N. (2023, May 1). *Dialectical behavior therapy (DBT): Definition, techniques, and benefits.* Verywell Mind. www.verywellmind.com/dialectical-behavior-therapy-1067402

Social anxiety disorder. (n.d.). National Library of Medicine. https://www.ncbi.nlm.nih.gov/books/NBK327674/

Stinson, A. (2023, January 6). *What is box breathing?* Medical News Today. www.medicalnewstoday.com/articles/321805

Tanzini, L. (n.d). *Interesting facts about social anxiety.* Kinder in the Keys. kinderinthekeys.com/interesting-facts-about-social-anxiety/

Understanding the stress response. (2020, July 6). Harvard Health Publishing. www.health.harvard.edu/staying-healthy/understanding-the-stress-response

Volmar, M. (2018, June 7). *Twenty four ways the Internet is changing the world with positivity.* LinkedIn. www.linkedin.com/pulse/24-ways-internet-changing-world-positivity-marie-eva-b-b-volmar/

West, M. (2021, July 29). *What is the fight, flight, or freeze response?* Medical News Today. www.medicalnewstoday.com/articles/fight-flight-or-freeze-response

Williams, O.A. (2021, November 5). *118 private jets take leaders to COP26 Climate Summit burning over 1,000 Tons of CO2.* Forbes. www.forbes.com/sites/oliverwilliams1/2021/11/05/118-private-jets-take-leaders-to-cop26-climate-summit-burning-over-1000-tons-of-co2/?sh=208c16e953d9

www.ingramcontent.com/pod-product-compliance
Lightning Source LLC
Chambersburg PA
CBHW062018040426
42447CB00010B/2052